Dedicated to my late friends George Goldsmith-C
-who have inspired me to write.

# *Tales from around the Goodwin Sands*

**David Chamberlain**

By the same author :
Forgotten Shipwrecks of the Downs.
A heritage from the Goodwins.
The Goodwin Sands Man-of-War.



Published by Beaches Books
01304 362744

**ISBN 0-9548439-0-8**

*CONTENTS*

## *INTRODUCTION*

Almost every seafarer has heard of the Goodwin Sands and some can recount daring tales of the lifeboats and shipwrecks from the past. The ever changing ten miles of sand banks are still providing newsworthy items as they uncover history that has been buried for hundreds of years.

From the day they were formed, man has been losing vessels upon them. Some of these shipwrecks were quickly swallowed up in the shifting sand, yet, after many years of lying dormant, they are again laid bare. They emerge as complete time capsules and entombed in their hulls are the historic relics from antiquity, and occasionally the remains of their crew. The tide and the elements rapidly erode and disperse these artefacts and Britain's inheritance is lost forever.

For some, the Goodwin Sands are steeped in mysticism, and nobody has captured their atmosphere in print better than my late friend, George Goldsmith-Carter. His interest in pre-Christian religions and the occult has been woven into the legends that surround the Sands. There has never been a better book describing its moods than his, *The Goodwin Sands*, published in 1953.

George was a larger than life character, whose yarns would enthral everybody. He also had a wicked sense of humour, probably acquired from his many years of service on the Trinity House light ships. He must have had a good chuckle to himself, from whatever level of the astral plane that he is now on, when all of those people gathered in Deal to try and catch sight of the ghost ship, *Lady Lovibund*. It was his tale of love and dastardly deeds on the Goodwins over two hundred and fifty years ago, that led thousands to believe that the phantom ship appeared every fifty years. On Friday the 13th of February 1998, hundreds lined the seafront looking out to sea, with the belief that the spectre would be sighted. Many people still believe that the *Lady Lovibund* exists, although I am sure George had made the story up, as the ship's name does not appear in Lloyd's List. There will be, no doubt, many more thousands watching from Deal seafront on the next anniversary in the year 2048.

Combining fact with fiction makes for good reading, nevertheless, it also makes extra work for the serious researcher. By sifting through newspaper cuttings and books, one can ascertain how reality gets distorted. Any mistake the previous writer has included will be transferred by the next, and the truth will eventually become misshapen.

I have tried, after many years of enquiries, to hopefully have come to a fairly accurate conclusion to the many accounts that surround the shipwrecks. Also I have been lucky enough to come into contact with a handful of those involved. When the *Ross Revenge* went ashore on the Goodwins, I was recording all that happened. I felt the tug's master, Steve Parsons, did a great job in pulling her off, as I thought she would become a total loss. Meeting Captain Harmen Hieda fifty years after he saved the lives of the American sailors from their burning ship, *James Harrod*, was a great honour. At that time he was over eighty years old, yet as he related his brave deeds to me, his eyes shone with a youthful brightness and his memory was impeccable. Also David Aggett, who was only sixteen at the time, could reminisce on the stranding of the *Helena Modjeska* in 1945 as if it were yesterday.

Through the technology of the internet and emails, I have been in contact with two of the relations of the first officer of the *Stirling Castle*. Although one of them, Curtis, lives on the 'other side of the pond' his English cousin, Roger, has delved into their family history. They both carry the same surname as their great grandfather x 6, Benjamin Barnett, did. Although Benjamin lost his life on board the 70 gun man-of-war when she foundered on the Goodwins in 1703, it did not deter his son Curtis (which became a family name) from joining the navy in 1722. In just over twenty years, he rose to the rank of Commodore and Commander in Chief of His Majesty's East India Squadron.

The Bronze Age shipwreck site licensee, Alan Moat, gave me an interest in underwater archaeology and the dives I had with him at Langdon Bay, before he died, will always be fondly remembered. It has always been a mystery why such a vast amount (over 350) of Bronze Age axe heads, rapiers and spear heads were found on the sea bed. An investigation into their origin proved that some were of European source and many had been cut in pieces. It was surmised, rightly or wrongly, that there could have been a cross Channel trade in scrap metal three and a half thousand years ago.

Another protected wreck site licensee, Bob Peacock, has kindly involved me with the *Stirling Castle* on the Goodwins. Emerging from the sand lies the almost complete remains of an early eighteenth century warship. In recent years he has financed the whole project out of his own pocket. However, he feels that although the government expect restrictions and legislation, they will not fund any of Britain's heritage that can be lost through a storm or in the tide.

Although I know that my diving days are over, I have had the privilege of conversing with many of those who are still active in the sport. Between us, we have named some of the unknown wrecks that are positioned on the Admiralty chart of the Goodwins. From a recovered maker's plate, research can bring the dead ship alive. I have always found it fascinating how each historical fact and each newspaper cutting enables another piece of the jigsaw to fit together.

In the following tales, I have merely scratched the surface about the wrecks and their histories. I am sure that in the future, many more true stories will be collated from the area that surrounds the Goodwin Sands, the name that has brought fear to many a ship's captain.

The bell and bricks from the ketch ***Fearless***

***Stirling Castle*** starts to founder in the surf on the Goodwins

## *THE FINAL BERTH*

As the *Stirling Castle* came abreast of the newly built town of Lower Deal, preparations were being made to drop her anchor. The old war-ship was part of a squadron that had been on a campaign against the French in the Mediterranean throughout the summer. Under the command of Sir Cloudsley Shovell, the fleet had not been overly successful on their mission and the expedition was an ill-designed one. Some prizes had been taken and the blockading of Toulon was to keep the French fleet lying quietly at anchor. The Admiralty had under-victualled the ships, causing a loss of life and manpower which forced the vessels to return before they could create too much effect against the enemy.

The three hundred and sixty one suntanned officers and men shivered in the strong southwest wind on that cold day of the 17th of November, 1703. Captain John Johnson pulled his coat about himself as he watched his first officer organize the men at the cathead and cable locker. The captain felt apprehensive. The Goodwin Sands lay less than five miles offshore, along with the Brake Sands and other shoal water. Although the Downs was recognized as a good anchorage, it was also known for its strong tides which swept around the sand banks.

Under reduced canvas the, two-decked, 70-gun, third-rate man-of-war edged her way into the tide. As the seamen slackened off her braces the yards swung, releasing the wind from her sails. The best bower was let go from her starboard side and ten fathoms of thick hemp rope streamed through the hawsehole, before it went slack as the anchor hit the seabed. Whilst another twenty fathoms was let out, the rats, who out numbered the men, scuttled away to find another hiding place. The one thousand and eighty-seven ton ship was made fast and the wind-hardened canvas was lashed tightly to her spars. A pipe shrilled as the men, apart from the anchor watch, were stood down from their duties. They looked longingly at Deal before going below for their meagre meal of salt beef, hard biscuits and sour beer.

Throughout the following days the vessels laid at anchor in boisterous weather. With a new moon on the night of the 26th of November it was pitch black, also the tidal current was at its strongest on the midnight high tide. The gale of wind which had been blowing since the day before suddenly strengthened.

By one in the morning, the southwest wind had reached storm force and with the strong tide flowing in the same direction, most of the ships in the Downs started to drag their anchors. Those who had not already dropped their second one were now doing so.

Roy Kennet with some of the first finds from 1979

To the men on the *Stirling Castle* the screaming wind sounded akin to a bevy of Banshees. They had never heard the like of it before. Rigging and spars bowed before its force, and with a loud crack a mast split sending down an array of blocks and cordage about the deck and amongst the sailors. Volumes of seawater and spume cascaded over the bows, leaving the men disorientated and shivering. Every pump on the ship was clanking trying to deal with the ingress of water that was slowly filling the bilges of the warship.

Throughout the next two hours the bow look-out of those ships which still held fast were fearfully trying to peer through the maelstrom at the vessels that were dragging their anchors towards them. The *Stirling Castle* was one of those menaces.

At four a.m. the wind had increased to hurricane force, but the tide had slackened. The carpenters on the warship were cutting away masts that were still standing. The old ship was getting low in the water and the tremendous seas were still crashing on to her decks, which were littered with a mass of broken timber and cordage.

The men in the cable locker saw that the jerking motion of the anchor rope had lessened and the ship's anchors were starting to hold again.

The seamen below decks who had been relieved from the incessant and back-breaking pumping, lay breathless listening to the loud thumps on the hull as yet another wave hit the vessel. They were grateful for the darkness to hide the look of fear on their faces, as they knew that any minute the ship might founder on the Goodwins.

As another hour went by, the wind increased even more until, at times, it blew up to one hundred and fifty miles per hour. The ebb tide reluctantly started flowing the opposite way to the fury of south west wind, and with that combination, the sea became rougher than ever.

With the *Stirling Castle* occasionally holding at anchor, she struggled to turn into the tide, but rolled heavily in the troughs as the mountainous waves hit her beam on. It was impossible to stand unaided and men had already been lost overboard. The force of the wind on their faces took their breath away and felt like an unseen fist hitting them. They were exhausted, hypothermic and knew they could not survive much longer. Some of them prayed whilst others crawled to the officers wine stock, so they could spend their last hours in oblivion amongst the onion shaped bottles.

Suddenly those aboard the *Stirling Castle* felt the ship start to judder as she touched the sands at low tide. The hundred and thirty-three feet eleven inches of keel that John Shish of Deptford had laid twenty-four years previously, was now digging a furrow into an outcrop of the Goodwin's known as the Bunt Head. In this shoal water the tide was slack and the sea was not as rough, but it was to be her final berth.

It would not be until forty-eight hours later, when the seas had calmed down, that only eighty men were rescued from the stern of the derelict hulk before she was engulfed by the high tide.

The angle at which the shipwreck of the *Stirling Castle* laid enabled the tide to scour out the sand and settle her deeper into the Goodwins, thus burying the remains and memories of one of the 'Great Storm' wrecks.

It was in the summer of 1979, after another sand shift, that the wreck became exposed and was re-discovered by divers. It was revealed to be an archaeological treasure chest. Much of her navigational equipment and armament was still in situ, along with the crew's personal effects. She presented an enclosed time capsule from Queen Anne's navy.

The next year the divers realised that the Goodwins had yet again consumed the wreck, but managed to find two other men-of-war from the same storm. Whilst checking the site in 1998, the current protected wreck site licensee, Bob Peacock, found she had become exposed from the sand wave. From the following year up to the present time, they have been surveying her remains before she disintegrates and is lost forever.

One of the ***Stirling Castle's*** large cannons

## *TREASURE ON THE GOODWINS*

The topping out ceremony of the new East India Docks was a lavish affair. Many of the dignitaries wore their finest clothing and the gowns of their ladies were of quality and the latest style. Food and drink were in abundance as the sun beat down on that hot August day in 1806. It reflected off the new paintwork of the two ships that had entered the dock. These vessels were the *City of London* and the nine-year-old *Admiral Gardner*, both ships belonging to the Honourable East India Company (HEIC).

The *Admiral Gardner* proudly flew the British Anchor at her foremast top, the Royal Standard at her main and the Union Flag on the mizzen. Displayed from the lower rigging were the flags of all the nations, but with the French colours at the base. The 32-gun vessel was there to be honoured for her actions against the far more powerful *Bellona*. With her twelve gun ports showing from the middle deck and eleven on the upper it was obvious, with her rich cargoes, she had to be an efficient fighting ship as well as merchantman.

She had a narrow beam of 36 feet, compared to the vessel's length of 145 feet and it

Deal boatmen save most of the ***Admiral Gardener's*** crew

proved that she was a fast ship. Her burthen of 816 tons enabled plenty of cargo space throughout her three decks.

As the *Admiral Gardner* lay basking in the warmth of that glorious summer's day, those attending did not know the fate that she would suffer in less than two and a half year's time.

Loading the ship took almost a month to complete. Food stores for the long voyage were of the utmost importance and they were always superior to naval victuals. The cargo was mainly iron goods, comprising of cannon balls, anchors, door-locks and nails. Tons of copper ingot slabs, cast by the Rose Copper Company of Redruth, also made their way into the lower decks. Hundreds of small wooden barrels, containing coins cast at the Soho

Mint, Birmingham, were stacked on top of each other in the holds.
The 46 tons of copper specie, almost a year's mintage, had the appearance of a token. On the obverse side the coat of arms of the East India Company was displayed, along with the date of mint, 1808. The reverse side showed inscriptions in Persian, the diplomatic language that was used in the Mughal India and at the bottom the denomination was displayed, X cash or XX cash. There were approximately 28,000 coins stored in each cask.
When Captain William John Eastfield was satisfied that everything was in order he reported to the H.E.I.C that the *Admiral Gardner* was ready to start the voyage. They informed him that he was to sail with two other outward bound Indiaman, the *Britannia*, a larger ship of 1,200 ton whose decks contained more cargo but fewer cannons, and the new *Carnatic*.
Leaving the Thames, Captain Eastfield briefly docked his ship into Gravesend and picked up some passengers and a Channel Pilot. The coldness of January 1809 was hoped to be soon forgotten in the hotter climes of Bengal and the Indian Ocean. As the *Admiral Gardner* and her consorts entered the Downs on the night of the 24th, they were greeted by a strong gale from the southwest. The pilot thought it would be wiser to ride the storm out under canvas than anchor in the darkness amongst the other vessels.
When the wind backed to the northwest it strengthened and the coldness numbed the crew's bodies to the core. By then the pilot realised the little fleet of ships had been driven out of the anchorage and close to the Goodwin Sands. Two anchors on each vessel were hastily dropped with the heavier *Britannia* letting go a third. The men beat their hands together to get back some feeling before they climbed the icy rigging to take in the small amount of canvas that was still hoisted. The sails were almost frozen, and as the seamen fisted and lashed them up to the vibrating spars, they could hear the thundering surf of the Goodwins above the howling wind. By the taffrail a sailor was swinging a lead, his face smarting as the rainsqualls lashed him. His soundings were relayed back to the pilot and captain by apprehensive crew members. From fourteen fathoms to ten the ships slowly dragged anchors towards their ultimate danger. Even through the darkness, waves could be seen breaking and cascading high in the air on the sands.
Unbeknown to the East Indiamen, another tragedy was being played close by. The large brig, *Apollo,* was in the same predicament as the other vessels. Her master, Captain Riddall, decided to take a chance and leave his doomed ship, before she was lost on the sandbank. Eighteen crewmen helped him launch the ship's longboat into the fury. Only one man, who was too terrified to leave the rigging, stayed to watch, as the boat was swamped and sank, taking his companions with it beneath the surging sea.
The *Admiral Gardner* and *Britannia* were perilously close to the surf but they thought their anchors were starting to hold. By 6:30 in the morning the *Admiral Gardner's* seamen became hypothermic and were fatigued, but they slowly relieved the ship of any canvas that she still flew. In an attempt to hasten the procedure, the pilot ordered the main sheet to be cut away. As he assisted the men, hacking away with their knives, he lost two of his fingers. In those circumstances it was almost a minute before he realised what had happened. Shock soon overcame him and he was carried below, delirious, leaving the captain in charge as the weather conditions worsening.
With heavy seas hitting the vessel, a large wave swept through the length of the upper deck and a sailor was washed overboard. Courageously, the third mate and three seamen embarked in the ship's boat in an attempt to save him, but they soon disappeared, never to be seen again.
The Quarter Master called out that the leadsman only had seven fathoms on his line and

then five. As Captain Eastfield instructed the carpenters to cut away the main and mizzenmast, the ship struck the sands.

The sky, on that Wednesday morning, was the same dark grey as the sea and only the white surf broke the illusion that it was joined. The hulks of the two East Indiamen and the Brig were lying close to each other, with seas crashing over their decks. Each of the vessels had only their foremast left standing, and upon them were hoisted signals of distress. The crews were huddled together on the poop decks in total despair.

Deal boatmen, from the cliffs south of Kingsdown, observed the shipwrecks. It had not been possible for them to launch their boats until the tide had changed. When the wind turned to the north and the sea moderated, late in that cold afternoon, they managed to get alongside the three derelict ships. They successfully rescued the remaining seamen from the Indiamen and the sole survivor off the *Apollo*.

Very little salvage took place over the following week, as most of the cargo was deep in the holds, which were underwater at all states of the tide. Although the value of both ship's cargoes was over £200,000, only the *Britannia* was insured, for £7,000. Eventually the pounding surf broke up the wrecks, until no trace of them could be seen.

It was not until 1982, that the wreck was again found by an unwary Ramsgate trawler. The *St Richard*, skippered by Greg Allen, snagged his net in an area just off the west side of the Goodwins. When the divers went down to investigate, they could not believe their eyes. Amongst the exposed timbers they saw copper ingots, cannons and a few heavily encrusted and corroded coins.

Two years later the main caches of the coins were discovered in an overhang between the wreck's ribs. There were thousands upon thousands encased in casks and in pristine condition. Various means of salvaging were used, including controlled explosions, a pneumatic road drill and an airlift. The following year, the government declared the *Admiral Gardner* a protected wreck site in an emergency designation order, but not without a protest. It was the salvors who had objected to this order; their argument was that the wreck was outside the three-mile territorial limits, and they continued to salvage. It was not until 1989, that an extension to twelve miles enabled the nautical archaeologists to get the site re-designated; although by that time over one million coins had been lifted along with the copper ingots.

There were millions of coins in her holds

## *DEATH IN THE DOWNS*

The night of Saturday 26th of November, 1881, was to be bitterly remembered by Robert Wilds for the rest of his life. Wilds, the coxswain of the North Deal lifeboat, *Mary Somerville*, had heard talk in the town about his lack of courage. The weather that night had caused the loss of a ship and twenty-one seamen, yet the lifeboat did not go to their rescue. Rumours spoke of indifference to human suffering and cowardice. Through the columns of the letter page, in the local newspaper, Wilds stated the facts. 'The sea was so rough that the lifeboat was unable to launch and to have tried to do so would have been madness.' Wilds continued that there was a difference between daring and foolhardiness. His and his crew's families had to be considered and if any body could do a better job, he argued, then perhaps they should try. Robert Wilds died four years later; as coxswain of the lifeboat he had saved a total of two hundred and twenty-two lives, that had been put in peril, around the Goodwins and the Downs.

It was around midday on the Saturday that the ill-fated *British Navy* was being towed into the anchorage of the Downs. At forty minutes past noon the ship was at anchor, and as the Trinity House pilot left the vessel, he commented to the master, Captain Skelly, that the weather looked unpromising. By two in the afternoon, the wind had increased to gale force and that evening, according to the second officer, Rice Sibley, it blew a 'Perfect Hurricane'. Along with the south-south west wind there was intense rain and hail.

The *British Navy* was a iron sailing ship of 206 feet length, with a general cargo bound for Sydney, Australia. As the wind shrieked through her rigging, the more experienced hands considered the weather was more likened to that of Cape Horn. Five young apprentices, for whom this was their first voyage, were seriously reconsidering their choice of employment.

The sea in the Downs was becoming heavy and Captain Skelly ordered more chain to be released on the port anchor. At eleven-thirty that night, the chain cable parted. As the starboard anchor was let go, the ship snatched at the long length of links that were flowing from the hawse hole. She held for another hour until the surge of the monstrous seas again snapped that anchor chain. Skelly, with his ship drifting through the busy anchorage, told the crew to set the fore and main top mast stay sails and the jib to get her head before the wind. Within minutes the jib sheet was carried away and the vessel would not pay off. They hauled down the stay-sail and were about to brace the foreyard aback, when the ship hit the larger anchored vessel, *Larnaca*.

The full rigged iron sailing ship, *Larnaca,* shuddered as the 1,217 ton *British Navy* received the blow to her hull between the main and mizzen mast. Captain Skelly commanded his second officer to swing out the lifeboats. Again the vessel careened into the *Larnaca* with such force that she started to founder.

Below decks on the *British Navy* there was pandemonium. The bulkheads were caving in and there was an inrush of water. As the ship crashed against the *Larnaca*, she knocked two holes into the hull and carried away her head gear and starboard anchor. The noise of the two ships tearing each other apart coupled with the rage of the seas breaking over them, made the crews fight for survival. Adrenalin along with fear surged through the men as they realised that they were battling for their lives.

Blocks and rope were falling on to the deck of the *British Navy* as her spars swung about when the waves hit the ship. The lifeboats were thrown against the bulwarks and splintered into matchwood. As the tide ripped the two vessels apart, Rice Sibley jumped on to the *Larnaca*. In the confusion he found five more of his crew had done the same. They watched the doomed sailing ship clear their stern and sink on an even keel.

The strength of the wind did not let up, and within an hour the *Larnaca's* anchor, having been weakened by the collision, started to drag. She narrowly missed the wreck. Through the hail and rain, they could just make out the masts of the sunken ship and heard men shouting and from the main mast they could perceive a whistle being blown. Sibley remembered Captain Skelly requesting a whistle from him before his ship had hit the *Larnaca* a second time. They listened helplessly until the violence of the storm drowned out the calls for help. All around them other vessels were burning flares of distress.

At first light, the tug, *Cruiser,* managed to rescue the cook and two seamen off the forepart of the battered *British Navy* wreck. The majority of the crew, which included the apprentices and an unlucky *Larnaca* seaman who had jumped off his ship on to the *British Navy* when they had collided, had drowned.

As a reminder of the night's storm the wreck's masts showed above the surface and these were a danger to the other ships in the anchorage. Shortly after, Trinity House moored a lightship close by, to bring the attention to the shipping. The lightship crew had the job of rowing to the wreck's mast and placing on it a light through the hours of darkness. It was a chore they disliked and was dangerous in the winter weather. Six months later Alfred Gann and Co, of Whitstable, recovered some of the cargo and dispersed the wreck with the use of dynamite detonated by an electric charge from an accumulator.

Ninety years later, sports divers found a large bell on the wreck. When it was cleaned up, the name of *Larnaca* could clearly be seen. This caused some confusion to the divers, until they realised that an incredible phenomenon had occurred. The force of the collision had been so great that the bell had been violently transferred on to the deck of the *British Navy* just before she had sunk.

Disaster in the Downs

## *DOLPHIN DISASTER*

Even as the paddle wheels started to churn up the Thames mud, a light rain fell upon the river. The Watermen coiled up their heaving lines before going to the offices of the General Steam Ship Company to collect their dues from the pay clerk. It was 5:30 p.m. Thursday the 18th of September, 1885 and their days work was over.

The passengers on the *Dolphin* made their way to the small cabins which were situated just below deck. Captain John Elward pushed the ships telegraph to 'Half Speed Ahead' and black smoke poured out of the funnel, adding more pollution in the skies that surrounded the industrial Port of London. For the vessel, the ebb tide assisted a speedy passage towards the estuary and the shoal waters of the Nore. The master, who also held a pilots licence, knew of all the dangerous sand banks through the inshore shipping lane well.

Just before darkness, the wheelhouse door was closed to keep out the chill of a north-easterly which had freshened with the persistent rain. As Elward thrust his hands into the pockets of his reefer jacket, he briefly checked the compass course that the helmsman was steering.

The galley was hot with the food being prepared for the thirteen passengers and twenty-five crewmen. With five women amongst the passengers the stokers were warned to keep their curses down to a minimum. In the holds of the paddle steamer was a general cargo, along with 300 barrels of sherry. Her destination was the French port of Le Havre.

At midnight the Chief Mate, Amos Seldon, took over the middle watch. He handed a mug of tea to the master and chatted to him about the inclement weather. As they approached the *Gull Lightship* the captain left the bridge and retired to the chart room to rest. He noted that the time was 1:15 a.m. and he had been on duty for over eight hours.

The *Dolphin* was now steaming, at full speed, through the buoyed inshore shipping lane towards the Downs.

Around about the same time the 1,641 ton *Brenda*, of West Hartlepool, bound for London with a cargo of cotton and grain, had just passed the South Foreland. The new watch had made sure that her navigation and steaming lights were bright and the lamps had sufficient oil in them. On the bridge was Captain John Merryfield. He had been in deep conservation with the Pilot since they had picked him up off Dungeness Point. The night was very dark and the rain and wind made vision difficult. A sailing ship passed 200 yards on their starboard side and ahead they saw two ships approaching them. The first ship passed at least a quarter of a mile clear but the second one appeared to be on a collision course.

Onboard the *Dolphin* seaman William Hamilton was at the wheel, and it was he who told Seldon of the situation and the close proximity of the large ship that lay ahead. As the chief mate peered through the bridge window a heavy rain squall almost obliterated his view. He felt the vessel surge in the following sea and ordered the helmsman to steer a little more to port.

The pilot and captain of the *Brenda* could not believe their eyes as the paddle steamer altered course across their bows. Merryfield commanded his helmsman to put the wheel to starboard and gave one blast on the ships whistle. Although he expected the *Dolphin* to then turn to starboard he was appalled when the little ship held her course. The pilot pulled the lever of the telegraph back until it registered 'Stop' and then 'Full astern' and sounded the steam whistle three times. He shouted to the seaman to 'go hard a port' as the vessel reduced her speed to almost two knots. The 257 foot ship merely caressed the side of the *Dolphin*, but it was enough to put a gash in her from the keelson to the deck, just abaft the paddle wheel.

Women screamed at the sound of the metal plates being ripped out of the ship. The massive bow of the *Brenda* intruded into their cabins. As she slowly pulled off, the paddle steamer's wheels thrashed the water in a fury of foam. Men and women were hurrying to reach the deck as the vessel started to settle by the stern, whilst Captain Elward had rushed to the bridge on the impact of the collision. He had no need for an explanation as he watched the bow of the *Brenda* disappear into the darkness. Amongst the chaos the seamen were making the life boats ready and some of the passengers, in different stages of dress stood by calmly. Elward noticed the ship engines were still going full ahead and steered his ship towards the dim shape of land. From the bridge the chief mate hurriedly set off eight rockets, which were barely visible in the gloom. As the ship settled lower in the water the paddle wheels started to labour and her speed lessened.

Into the engine room water flowed until, within four minutes, it had put out the boilers fire. The stokers and donkeymen rushed up the companionway ladder closely followed by steam and smoke. As the *Dolphin's* two cylinder compound engine died, the lifeless hull came to a standstill less than a mile from shore.

With the loss of momentum the vessel quickly started to sink. In less than half an hour the sea was almost up to her gunnels and two life boats were launched. As she slowly slipped beneath the waves, those that were left onboard raced to the highest part of the ship, the wheelhouse-roof and mast. For a few minutes the buoyancy inside the wheelhouse kept the *Dolphin* from completely submerging and the survivors frantically searched for better hand holds. With a loud report the bolts were ripped out of the deck and the whole of the structure floated clear as the vessel sank.

Alerted by some of the rockets, a boatman from the beach at Kingsdown had launched his galley. As he came upon the scene he realised that he had not been summoned for a service but was a witness to a disaster. Fearing the survivors would sink his small boat he returned ashore to alert the Kingsdown Lifeboat crew.

Meanwhile the fresh north-east wind chopped up the waves as the flood tide flowed

The ***Brenda's*** bow sliced into the ***Dolphin***

against it. The cold wind started to chill the bodies of the survivors as they waited for salvation. A woman screamed pitifully as she was swept off the half submerged wheelhouse-roof. Nobody could help her and mercifully there was silence within seconds.

The boatman had difficulty in raising the crew that early in the morning. It was at five o'clock, two and a half hours later, before the lifeboat, *Charles Hargrave*, along with two galleys, managed to get to the wreck and rescue the first of the casualties. They found the captain and his chief mate, Amos Seldon, along with two seamen clinging to the rigging, which was attached to the *Dolphin's* mast 18 feet above the water. A French passenger was found straddled over the funnel, which was barely showing above the sea, and an unconscious man, who had lashed himself to the rail on the wheelhouse-roof with his handkerchief, barely alive.

A steam gauge from the ***Dolphin***

Eight people (four passengers and four crew men) were lost and those who survived were brought ashore in a wretched condition.

At the inquest the master and pilot of the *Brenda* were exonerated unlike the chief mate of the *Dolphin*. He was blamed for the collision, but as he and the captain had stayed with the vessel, as she sank, the court allowed him to keep his officers certificate. The reason the *Brenda* left the other sinking vessel was because she had been badly damaged in her bow and there was a concern that she would also sink. The ship had slowly made her way back to Dover for repairs.

The barrels of liquor were salvaged promptly, to take temptation away from the local boatmen, and the 641 ton wreck was blown up; clearing the remainder of the hulk, that was situated close to the shipping lane.

# *FLOATING FURNACE*

It was by the cold light of dawn that one hundred and fifty passengers from the Hamburg-American liner *Patria* abandoned ship. There was no panic, Captain Frohlieh and his officers supervised the evacuation and everything had been well organized. The passengers had been awoken at 6 a.m. on that Wednesday morning of the 15th November, 1899 and were told to go, with haste, to their lifeboats stations. Some with only blankets draped over their nightclothes and others, in various states of dress, had no need to speculate the cause for concern. As they mustered around the steamships eighteen lifeboats, smoke could be seen pouring out from the ships holds. Part of the *Patria's* cargo of wax and linseed was well ablaze. Standing by the burning ship were the vessels *Ceres*, *Athesia* and the Ramsgate fishing smack *Adieu*. They had been alerted by the flames coming from the vessel and helped in the rescue of the passengers.

The *Patria* had almost completed the last stage of her long voyage from America to Hamburg. Her position was a few miles from the *North Hinder lightship*; close to home but not close enough. As the day progressed, acrid smoke started to engulf the bridge, Captain Frohlieh ordered the rest of his crew to take to the safety of the lifeboats and awaiting ships.

Throughout the night he, with four of his officers and a few volunteers, remained fighting

Hamburg-American liner ***Patria***

the fire. They did so until the wind shifted and the flames started to creep to the ship's stern, where they were struggling with the pumps. When the heat became unbearable they also abandoned the *Patria* and boarded the *Athesia* - which had stood by the floating furnace all night. After an assessment on Thursday morning the exhausted captain realised he could do nothing more. With reluctance he proceeded towards Hamburg in the *Athesia*, leaving the blazing ship drifting in the North Sea. As they approached Cuxhaven the Hamburg-American company tug *Hansa* was sighted and Captain Frohlieh was transferred aboard her. After a brief discussion it was decided to steam, at full speed, in search of the now abandoned vessel.

Eventually, at eight on Saturday morning, they sighted the still alight *Patria* some distance from the *East Goodwin light vessel.* As the *Hansa* approached she found two British steamers standing by the abandoned ship - they had tried towing her but their hawsers had snapped under the strain and heat. As the tug went alongside the *Patria* the crew were amazed to see six French fishermen perched on her bows! They had boarded the fiery derelict in hopes of salvage, but were only too glad to be relieved of their temporary command for the safety of a cooler deck.
*Hansa* was joined by the German tug *Simson*, whose offer of help was gratefully accepted, as the towing of the 6,664 ton vessel in her present condition was going to be hard work. The tugboat skippers decided that the best course of action would be to tow her to Deal, and beach her in the sheltered waters of the Downs.
The tugs thick wire hawsers held as the liner approached land. Her hull above the water line glowed white with heat. Every part of the wooden decks and fittings had disappeared, and her heavy cargo and machinery, buckled by the fire, had shifted and caused a pronounced list to starboard. As she was being towed through the shipping lane, opposite Walmer Castle, the ship's hull burst. At 9:30 on Sunday morning and five days after she had caught fire, the *Patria's* stern sank to the seabed. Steam, smoke and sparks were seen to bellow from the ship for hours. Her two after masts toppled leaving only her funnel and forward mast preciously still standing - much to the bewilderment of the watching crowds, who had amassed along Deal's sea front.
Shortly after thick fog started to engulf the Downs in the cold but light November airs.
Within days the Yarmouth registered brigantine *Eleanor* had run into the part submerged hull of the *Patria.* The damage to the sailing ship's port quarter was so extensive she had to be towed to Dover for repairs. The owners of the *Eleanor*, faced with a large shipwright's bill, had an Admiralty writ placed on the remaining mast of the Patria; to try for some compensation for the damage occurred. To make sure nothing was touched until a settlement was made, a watchman was put in charge of the hulk. For him it was an uncomfortable job, at every high tide he would have to perch as far forward on the bows as possible and suffer the exposure of the Channel in winter. Under the charred and twisted remains of metal, iron beds and cooking utensils some of the valuable general cargo, amongst it being tons of copper, was still in the *Patria's* hold. A settlement was soon found, and as the customs officers removed the writ, the Copenhaven salvage vessel *Emzsvilzer* set about with her divers to try and patch up the holes in the wrecks hull.
As the fog cleared strong easterly winds briefly halted work on the burnt out shell. In the lulls of winter weather the salvors set about their task with fervour. The sound of explosions rocked Deal and Walmer as the salvage team removed the jigger and mizzenmast. These were still hanging over the submerged stern and hampered the divers progress. Also the Danish hard hat diver's skill and courage was greatly admired; to work in the dark murky waters which border the Goodwin Sands in the middle of December had to be tried to be appreciated.
For the men on the tugs, the heralding in of the new twentieth century was just another working day. On Wednesday 3rd January, 1900 the large Hamburg tugs *Albatross* and *Seeadler* were in position along side the wreck. As light faded Captain Spruth, the salvage master, and his divers were confident the *Patria's* holes had been patched up enough for a re-floating on the next day's high tide. The first glow of the weak sun lit the clamour of tugs and local boats as they bustled around the wreck. The pumps were rigged and started. On board the hulk were nearly twenty men. Some of them were the divers who had to unblock the suction pipe as it got choked up with part of the *Patria's* cargo of cooked, but soggy, grain and maize. Slowly the *Patria's* stern started to rise. The *Seeadler* had made

fast to the bow's of the ship and when her stern broke the surface the *Albatross* secured herself to it.

As the tide rose so did the blackened hull and shortly before noon the strong flood tide took possession of the powerful tugs burden. The *Patria* went out of control as her bow swung to the southeast, nearly capsizing the *Seeadler*. The two tugs struggled with the 490 feet long ship - although the hulk seemed to have a will of its own. Within fifteen minutes she had gone with the tide and without warning started to sink, this time by her bow.

Amongst the pandemonium loud reports were heard, as her bulkheads and plates gave way. It happened quickly; the ship completely disappeared under the water leaving all the men on deck struggling in the sea. Owing to the time of year many wore heavy clothing and leather sea boots - their salvation had to be quick or they would be dead. The local boats and tugs were prompt and did a good job amongst the chaos in saving most of the lives. Those who did not stand a chance were the chief diver Leopold Halfried who was pulled under whilst sitting in a small boat, which was tied to the *Patria's* stern. He had full diving dress on apart from his brass helmet. Also two other divers and two local men perished. Every effort was made to retrieve the drowned men and they searched for the others until all were accounted for.

At the inquest Captain Spruth, the salvage master, was exonerated from any blame. He stated that he thought the ship would have floated after the repairs, and had used two of Germany's most powerful tugs. Additionally he had consulted local knowledge on the tides. It was a mystery, why had she sunk? After a two week clearing up period the tugs had secured their pumps and other gear and left the Downs.

Throughout the summer months a Whitstable salvage company took over the wreck, recovering the copper and most of the other non-perishable cargo. Amongst the debris they found a grim reminder of the tragedy, the lead sole of one of the divers boots.

It was then left to Trinity House authorities to disperse the wreck and make it safe for future shipping using the channel. This they did at a reputed cost of £6,000 and on the 2nd January 1902 the wreck marking lightship was removed from the site.

Danish divers working in freezing conditions

## *A TRAGEDY OF ERRORS*

The captain of the SS *Mahratta* looked wearily at the calendar on the bulkhead of his stateroom; it read 9th April, 1909. Thirty-five days earlier they had left Calcutta with passengers and a general cargo to the value of £150,000. In her holds were tea, jute, hemp, rice, hides and spices. They had also taken on more tea and rubber at Ceylon. As he stared at the calendar, almost mesmerized, he knew something was not quite right about it. He was damned if he could fathom out what it was!

He knew every part of the 5,730-ton ship from almost the day that she had been built in 1892. When the Brocklebank Line had first commissioned the *Mahratta,* he had been aboard her as a young ambitious fourth officer. All of his seafaring life he had worked for the company, as did his father before him. He had fond memories throughout those years as he gained yet another gold ring on his jacket sleeve, which enabled him to climb another rung up the ladder to achieving his masters' ticket.

As Captain Ellery's bloodshot eyes dropped to the ship's log, the calendar tilted another quarter of an inch. The man had only snatched three hours sleep in the last forty since they had passed Ushant. He silently read the entry from the log, wishing he could tear out the page and rewrite it. The copperplate writing was in the hand of his second officer Albert Day, a man whom he liked and trusted. Day had just gained his masters certificate and was awaiting a position to become vacant so he could take up his first command; but now that wait would take many years longer. The initial entry had read

*12:15.a.m. Captain Ellery has turned in after spending 36 hours on the bridge, I (the second officer) and the Trinity House pilot, Mr. Finnis, are in command. We have just sighted Dungeness. Sea calm, moderate northwest breeze, visibility 8 miles and ships speed 10 knots. 2:38.a.m. South Foreland light sighted no change in sea conditions. 2:58.a.m. I have sighted a flashing light and have tried to point it out to the pilot. 3:10.a.m. The pilot has acknowledged the flashing light on our port beam but cannot identify it. 3:15.a.m. The ship has run aground; pilot has given orders for engines to be stopped. 3:20.a.m. We have identified the flashing light, it is the Gull Lightship; therefore we are aground on the Goodwin Sands* - the next lines were in the captain's hand. *3:25.a.m. Have taken over the bridge and have sent for the chief engineer to inquire about more steam. The Lightship on our port beam is firing rockets and a signal gun to alert shore assistance, but we are in no danger. 3:32.a.m. Second officer has just informed me that he has found the chief engineer dead with his throat cut.*

It was now 7a.m. and Captain Ellery closed the log and looked out of the porthole. He could just make out the lifeboats from Deal, Ramsgate and Broadstairs alongside his ship; also there were the tugs *Lady Crundal* and the *John Batley.* After a knock on the cabin door his attention was averted as the coxswain of the Deal lifeboat entered. Captain Ellery noted his weather beaten features and knew here was a man who worked hard and often around these dreaded Goodwins.

The Coxswain, William Adams, inhaled the aroma of tea and spice; the smell was unnatural to his nostrils. As he looked around the neat cabin he noticed that the calendar on the bulkhead was tilting. He expressed concern that such a large ship as the 446 feet long *Mahratta* was on a bad part of the sandbank. He instructed the captain to employ all the aid offered to tow the ship off as soon as possible, as the tide would soon scour the sand at the bow and stern which would then cause her back to break. Also if he and his crew were to stand by, would it be possible for hot food and drink to be provided from the *Mahratta's* galley?

Ellery was now at the end of his tether, how dare a rough boatman give him advice on how to save his ship! He also had better things to do than feed this mans crew. It was the last request and advice William Adams was to give the captain, he left the ship to return to the lifeboat.

After a futile attempt to get himself off the sand bank on the morning's tide, Captain Ellery reluctantly employed the two tugs for £1,000, on a 'no cure no pay' clause. They were joined by another six tugs and another agreement was made for an extra £5,000. As the eight tugs set about their work, straining to pull the *Mahratta* off, many of the Deal beach boats were gathering around the ship. Some of the skippers were just watching whilst others were offering advice and assistance. Captain Ellery's patience was again wearing thin as he was informed that the tugs labours were unprofitable and when, finally, one of the small boats brought out police Inspector Hayward the captain's mood became noticeably more sullen.

The policeman went most minutely into the facts of the death of the chief engineer. It

Tugs attempt to pull the ***Mahratta*** off the sand bank.

appeared that when the *Mahratta* had passed Portland the pilot had boarded bringing mail. A letter was addressed to the chief engineer and was thought to have been from his wife - although no sign of this letter could be found. The body of Samuel Gibson, aged 35, was discovered by the second officer who tripped over Gibson's inert legs when he had gone to summon him for the captain. He stated that the body was cold and he surmised that the officer had been dead for some time. It also appeared that Gibson had stood before the mirror, in his cabin, and cut his own throat. The captain could not give Hayward an explanation why his engineer had done this, although a stoker had said his chief was depressed since he had received his letter. No reason could be given for his death but a request to take the body ashore was refused. Captain Ellery felt certain his ship would be towed off on Saturday's tide and the dead man would be landed at Tilbury on Sunday.

As the inspector left, fourteen of the passengers followed him to board the lifeboat and were landed on the beach at 6 p.m. Within the hour, the lifeboat *Charles Dibden* was back along side the *Mahratta*. Coxswain Adams knew it was only a matter of time before he

would be needed again.
That night, at high water, sparks could clearly be seen coming from the funnels of the eight tugs as they struggled with their burden. Their efforts were yet again in vain, the *Mahratta* did not move an inch. In the early hours of Saturday morning, all of the salvage masters decided that a lot of cargo had to be removed before another attempt to refloat her could be made. At daybreak, an armada of the little Deal boats brought out over a hundred men. Their job was to lighten the ship and two hundred tons of jute was thrown overboard into the sea. There was also a large barge secured along side the *Mahratta*, into it part of her more valuable cargo was being offloaded.
All of the salvors realised that time was now running against them. The ship was starting

The last to leave was a black cat

to make groaning noises and was taking on a noticeable list. It was going to be in their best interests to make every effort, on the next tide, to get her free from the ever-increasing grasp of the Goodwins.
For three fruitless hours the eight tugs pulled and on the falling tide they reluctantly cast off their non-obliging tow. As the flotilla steamed away from the Goodwins to the safety of the Downs, they anchored opposite Deal pier. Anglers and onlookers watched as shortly after the arrival of the tugs a local boat landed the body of Samuel Gibson (who eventually was to be buried in the local cemetery) and the haggard looking Captain Ellery.
His stay was brief; that evening a message was sent to the captain to return to his ship as she was starting to break up. When he arrived along side the *Mahratta* he viewed a four-foot gap amidships, her back had finally snapped. The second officer explained to him of the panic as she split. He stated that the rivets were flying about like hail, and the crew of 67 Lascars had jumped into the lighter, which was still moored alongside, and would not re-board her. Captain Ellery half-heartedly tried to convince the Indians that there was no danger; but after seeing the look of abject terror in their faces he agreed for them and the barge to be towed back to Dover.
With the arrival of daylight on Easter Sunday, Captain Ellery and Second Officer Day could see that no more could be done and left with the other officers on a final trip back to

Deal. On the way back he could not bring himself to look at the now broken remains of his beloved ship. He could also not bear to make eye contact with the weather beaten lifeboat Coxswain. William Adams had stood by the vessel (on and off) for a total of 50 hours, and had rescued a total of 38 people before the *Mahratta* was totally abandoned.

With the barometer dropping and freshening winds, the Liverpool Salvage Association took over the wreck. They made a deal with many of the local boats, that for all that was salved, they would get paid a third of the value. Unfortunately the Deal boatmen were well known for their rascally ways and most of the cases of tea did not arrive at the warehouse. The salvage company alerted the police who decided to raid the homes of the boatmen. The longshoremen were tipped off and many dumped the tea down the manholes and into the main drains of Deal. Another decided to fill his bed-ridden grandmother's mattress full of tea, unfortunately for him, when the police knocked at his door, his granny took fright and became incontinent. Later when it rained the whole of Deal and Walmer's drains were blocked with the swelling tealeaves and many a cellar was flooded. Only one man was found in possession of two cases of tea, which weighed 170lb and was fined £20.

Within the week more gales widened the split in the *Mahratta's* 49-foot beam, and her bridge was only just showing at high water. Days later a small black cat was found and rescued from the almost submerged hulk. It was to be the last living thing that came off the wreck, which was sucked beneath the sea seven days after she had struck the infamous Goodwin Sands.

Although the wrecking of the *Mahratta* could possibly have been averted, it could hardly be comprehended that in 1939 a sister ship, owned by the same company and also with the same name, would come to grief a mere three quarter of a mile away. It was a very curious coincidence!

Again the Goodwins swallow another victim

The ***Preussen*** in full sail

## *THE KAISER REGRETS*

On the morning of November 15th, 1910, the wind had fallen light and a sea mist was engulfing the English Channel. The mighty becalmed *Preussen* needed the assistance of a tug to tow her up-channel. She was the largest full rigged sailing ship in the world, 5,081 tons and a length of 433 feet. This vessel could also boast that her spread of canvas was twice as great as any British sailing ship. When her 48 sails were set, she showed 59,000 square feet of canvas which was controlled by 26 miles of wire and rope. But without wind - she was as helpless as a fish out of water in these Channel tides.

The *Preussen* was part of the Flying P Line, of which there were 14 other sailing ships all based at Hamburg. Her owner was Reederi F. Laeisz, who was a man of tradition and had not invested in steam ships which were now taking over the trade routes around the world. Yet he had been successful enough in his business to keep his large sailing ships working, amongst them being the *Potosi* of 4,025 tons, the *Pamir* 3,020 tons and the ill fated *Preussen.*

Captain Heinrick Nissen had made sure the 5,000 tons of general cargo had been stowed correctly as the voyage to Valparaiso, passing Cape Horn, would be a long and hard one. Early that following morning, when nearing Newhaven, a steady breeze from the south-south-west had arisen, and the *Preussen* slipped the tug's tow. Setting all her sails, she made an impressive sight as she leapt through the water in the slowly clearing sea mist.

Although the captain of the ss *Brighton* (the Newhaven - Dieppe ferry) had seen the large sailing vessel approaching, he misjudged her speed as he tried to pass ahead of her bows. The tearing and rasping of the *Preussen's* rigging as it raked the ferry's port side must have been frightening to the *Brighton's* 90 passengers; it damaged the foremast, funnel and lifeboats. However, the collision had left the sailing ship in a crippled condition smashing her jib-boom and shrouds. As the ferry returned the five miles back to

Newhaven the wind freshened to gale force.

Captain Nissen, not wanting to risk his masts, was towed to Dungeness where he dropped both anchors hoping to ride out the storm force winds. But owing to the strength of wind and tide the *Preussen*, with her weakened bow, lost her anchors and chain. They had to employ three tugs, which pulled her up through heavy seas towards Dover, where hopefully she could be secured to one of the large mooring buoys in the harbour. When the tugs tried to manoeuver her towards the harbour entrance she became unmanageable as the conditions worsened and, after a while, more tugs came out from Dover to assist, but to no avail.

Aground at Fan Bay

At half past four that afternoon, she parted her tow ropes and went aground at Fan Bay, a mere mile from the safety of the harbour. Within half an hour a distress flare had been fired and the Dover Lifeboat struggled out of the entrance of the harbour towards the stranded vessel. Above, on the cliffs, men from the Coast Guard rescue unit, complete with protective wicker headgear and rocket apparatus, were painfully climbing down the chalk cliff face. Unfortunately their rope was twenty feet too short which made the decent to the beach twice as difficult and dangerous.

When the lifeboat approached the stricken ship, the crewmen could see none of the *Preussen's* forty-eight crew and two passengers. There were no willing hands to secure the rope which had been shot across the vessel's rigging by the shore party and, as it was low water, the lifeboat had to stand off the stranded vessel from fear of going aground herself. Apart from lights in the cabins and sparks from the galley chimney, no signs of life could be seen and the would-be rescuers returned home puzzled.

By five o'clock the next morning, the gale had abated slightly and four tugs attempted to pull her off. Their efforts were unsuccessful and the vessel was starting to dig her own grave in the soft chalk seabed. It was evident that she would not move until her holds had been lightened, and Captain Nissen was taken ashore to consult her owner and agents for the best course to take on the mishap. As soon as the Captain reached land, the gale suddenly arose again, leaving him stranded and unable to get back to his ship. All he could do was watch helplessly as twelve tugs struggled to pull the stranded *Preussen* off at high water, until they abandoned their task at 2 p.m.; the ship not having budged an inch!

When asked, Captain Nissen explained to the interested the reason for the crew not wanting to be rescued by the lifeboat. It was because they had all come to the conclusion that the vessel was sound and if she should start to break up they could easily swim ashore.

Even with 14 feet of water in the fore-hold and sea running in and out of the bow, the gallant crew could be seen cheerily waving to the spectators, who were lining the edge of the cliffs. The following day as the gale died down, thirteen of the youngest crewmen and both of the passengers were taken ashore. One of the passengers professed that he was a seascape artist, and after this eventual voyage he would have enough ideas to paint for the rest of his life.

It was found that the ship's hull had settled into five feet of chalk, and the sails were taken off her yards for the last time. Just before the remainder of the reluctant crew left the ship, Captain Nissen read out a telegram he had received from the Kaiser. It expressed his deepest regrets to the owner for the loss of such a great ship from the German merchant fleet. It was now up to the salvage company to save the merchandise from below her decks.

The deserted deck

The coming month was a difficult one for her salvors. They managed to transfer most of her cargo onto lighters. However, owing to the winter weather and the variation of goods in her holds, things did not go smoothly. She carried grand pianos, cement, china cups and saucers, coke, even salt and pepper cruet sets. A last and final attempt was undertaken to tow her off, after dumping 500 tons of coke. This was unsuccessful and the ship was then left to the local boatmen to pick over the remains. At times this was quite lucrative as a sale in January 1911 fetched one skipper £200 on selling many hundredweights of paraffin wax, china and the ships steering wheels. The spring gales battered the hulk and an attempt to break her up as scrap was abandoned late that summer.

When her anchors were recovered from the sea at Dungeness and landed on the harbour wall at Dover, it was speculated they were the largest ever to be seen at that port. Winter came and the once proud *Preussen* broke up leaving only her ribs protruding from the sea, a condition which has altered little since then, and her remains can still be seen at low water to this present day.

## *SILENT SERVICE*

The collision had not been felt by the hundreds of passengers on the 22,621 ton German Atlantic liner *Amerika*. Some were starting to dress for breakfast although many were still asleep in their bunks. A few were on deck, at six o'clock on that morning of the 4th of October, 1912, as it would have been a chance to view the important Admiralty Harbour of Dover. The dark war clouds of the two mighty nations were drawing together; the British bulldog was becoming wary of the Prussian eagle's increasing sea power. It was not unusual for Hamburg vessels, bound for America, to slowly pass close to Dover and collect any last orders or mail. With each visit the captain of the *Amerika* had seen a greater build up of warships from the port than the time before. He had also noted a lot more activity with naval manoeuvres. Fortunately the fast destroyers had always given the lumbering passenger ship a wide berth.

With the *South Goodwin lightship* on his starboard beam he had hardly noticed, almost

There was only one survivor from the ***B2***

directly below his bow, the small cigar-shaped object surface; it was barely recognizable amidst the tumbling seas in the first light of the morning. Seconds before the collision occurred, the German captain had ordered 'hard-a-starboard', but it was too late - the liner hit the 150 foot submarine amidships. The *B2* merely bounced off the great liners bows, leaving a hole six feet by two feet through which sea water had gushed in.

Before she cleared the *Amerika's* stern, the submarine sank. Some of the passenger-ship's crew threw life-buoys into the sea. The captain sounded four and then three blasts on his steam whistle and ordered flares to be set off. Although all of these events had happened in minutes - the ship made no attempt to stop, and heartlessly carried on her course.

Lieutenant Richard Pulleyne was about to realise the fear of every sailor: the dread of drowning. On the impact of the collision, he fell from the conning tower and on to the deck below. It was all happening very quickly! The submarine had just surfaced, and the crew of sixteen felt her pitch and roll in the heavy seas that the fresh north-east wind had created. As Pulleyne hit the gratings, his submarine was being pushed over at right angles. He heard the noise of metal being ripped open and saw the lights go out. Straight away daylight entered the darkness, but in an instant the cold morning's air was replaced by freezing salt water.

As shadows again engulfed the *B2* he tried to struggle to his feet. All around him, and above the roar of the inrush of water, he could hear his crew-mates shouting. He felt the air being driven out past him and through the open hatch. The sub took less than a couple of minutes to reach the seabed in the sixteen fathoms of water. A pungent smell of chlorine gas burnt his throat and nostrils as the last vestige of air forced him through the narrow confines of the conning tower.

He felt calm, and resigned to die. Why struggle? Which way was up and which way down? Everything around him was dark and cold. Within a minute the air in his lungs would be replaced by water. After a few seconds of panic, it would be oblivion!

As his life's breath whistled from his lips he felt a terrible pain in his ears, but he noticed that around him it was getting lighter. He burst through the waves, like a Champagne cork out of a bottle, and thankfully gulped down the winter's air. He was alive!

It had been only minutes earlier that he had looked through the periscope and had seen no immediate danger in the choppy swell. The flood tide against the wind had caused the white capped waves. It was the captain who had ordered the conning tower hatch to be opened and their instructions were to make contact with the companion submarine, *C17.*

These were a new breed of seamen in a new type of vessel; the submersible. With their enthusiasm and youth they felt confident and almost indestructible. Throughout that week a whole flotilla of *B* and *C* type submarines had been practicing tactics in the Straits of Dover. Their audacity, in the buoyed roads of the Downs, was causing some near misses with the shipping. It was only owing to the small size of their craft that they luckily escaped the mishaps.

Lieutenant Pulleyne, the *B2's* second in command, had no idea what had happened. He was not only dazed but deaf. The pressure of one hundred feet of water had burst his ear drums. As he floundered in the sea he was positive that he would soon be picked up. With a flotilla of submarines in the area on exercises, plus other naval craft, he felt sure one of them must have seen the accident occurring. Unfortunately for him, it was half an hour later and one mile from the sinking, that Pulleyne was eventually dragged to safety by the crew of the submarine, *B16*. He was the only survivor found from the wreck.

Passengers on the 22,621 ton ***Amerika*** did not feel the collision

The Admiralty was prompt in issuing orders to search for the lost sub. Five pairs of destroyers, from the 6th flotilla, swept a six-by-two mile area of sea-bed. It was on that same Friday afternoon they thought they had found her, although disappointment was felt by the crews when, instead, a large rock broke the surface.
The following day's search only produced an anchor. It was not until Sunday afternoon that the three and a half inch wire, which the destroyers *Fairy* and *Leven* were towing, connected with the sunken hull. With daylight fading, marker buoys were placed around the wreck. Her position appeared to be further eastwards than first thought.
On Monday morning, the Dover Harbourmaster's divers descend into the murky waters above the wreck. They saw the hole near the conning tower but could not find any bodies. The brass helmeted divers managed to attach strops around the hull. These were connected to the hawser of the salvage vessel, lighter *No 94*. After three days of preparation, and just before they were about to start the lift, the Admiralty decided to abandon the project. They felt that, with the submarine's hull nearly cut in two, there could be a possibility that the wreck would disintegrate on the way up to the surface. If this did happen then it would bring more distress to all of those involved with the tragedy.
The destruction of the *B2* had become a national news item and the newspapers had followed the progress since the sinking. They had even hired some tugs to be at the funeral service which was to be held over the wreck on the following day. The cliff tops, along the South Foreland and St Margaret's Bay, were lined with people as the flotilla of ships slowly steamed to the submarine's resting place; three miles off land. As they approached the wreck buoy, a sea mist fell upon the site, shrouding and preserving the dignity of the fifteen men entombed in the *B2's* hull from the inquisitive onlookers.
Curiously a Dover boatman with the name of Brockman was very unhappy with the whole incident. He had witnessed the collision from his own craft and had declared that the *Amerika* had ploughed into the submarine. Angry Brockman felt the liner's captain did nothing beyond throw a few lifebuoys into the sea and fire a couple of rockets. He even boarded the ship to reprimand her captain, but was ordered off the bridge and back into his own vessel. He cursed the German's callousness; perhaps he was amongst the first to join the call to arms against them when Britain was plunged into war twenty months later.

The 3rd Portsmouth flotilla on manoeuvres at Dover

## *CRIPPENS' CURSE*

Captain Kendall had discreetly studied the odd couple who had boarded the Canadian Pacific Liner *Montrose.* On the passenger list their names were Mr. Robinson and son; however, Mr. Robinsons' boy looked and acted just too effeminate. Before his ship had steamed far into the Atlantic, he requested Marconi wireless operator Llewellyn Jones to send that famous Morse message to Liverpool. 'HAVE STRONG SUSPICIONS THAT CRIPPEN LONDON CELLAR MURDERER AND ACCOMPLICE ARE AMONG SALOON PASSENGERS. ACCOMPLICE DRESSED AS BOY MANNER AND BUILD UNDOUBTEDLY A GIRL.'

Shortly after the message was received, Chief Inspector Walter Dew boarded a much faster vessel, the White Star liner *Laurentic.* He arrived at Quebec before the other ship and made contact with the Royal Canadian Mounted Police. As the *Montrose* entered the St. Lawrence River, the policeman, who had disguised himself as a pilot, arrested Dr. Crippen and his mistress, Ethel Le Neve. Captain Kendall stood closely by with his pistol, as it was believed that Crippen was armed. As the doctor was led off the ship he turned and cursed Kendall for his initiative. Within ten months of murdering his wife, Hawley Harvey Crippen was himself hanged at Pentonville prison on a cold November morning in 1910.

Crippen's escape route, the ***Montrose.***

The 5,440 ton *Montrose* had been built in 1897, but at the approach of the Great War she was being superseded by the modern and faster ships that were plying the Atlantic route. It was for that reason the company put her up for sale. As hostilities were declared, the German U-boats caused havoc amongst the Allied shipping. With their successes they became more daring by approaching ever closer to the British shorelines. The Admiralty at Dover realised that their harbour, full of warships, would be a target. Their solution was that two strategically sunk block ships, at each entrance, would deflect a torpedo, but not hamper the comings and goings of a fleet. The 444 feet long *Montrose* was purchased by the Ministry of War Transport and moored against the Admiralty Pier in Dover Harbour. As she underwent alterations her superstructure was ripped away and many tons of ballast poured into her empty holds. They erected a line of pylons along the deck to secure the anti-torpedo nets. As she lay alongside the pier, hardly recognizable from her former glory, superstitious sailors and dockworkers deemed her as an unlucky ship. It was even said that if the *Montrose* was to be used, the war would go badly for the British.

Three days after the Christmas of 1914, a great storm swept up the Channel. Along with rain, the south-west wind reached 77 miles per hour and made the sea conditions evil. The *South Goodwin lightship* was the first casualty of this gale and her anchor started to drag as the weather worsened. Her rockets of distress were seen and North Deal lifeboat was made ready to launch. With the help of the haul off rope, and four men almost up to their armpits in water holding the greenheart skids, Coxswain Adams successfully pulled the lifeboat through the surf.

That night, as the storm raged on, the high spring tide filled Dover Harbour. The *Montrose* snatched at her ropes and eventually broke away from her moorings. With the haven full of warships, she miraculously drifted past all of them without doing any damage. In a shower of sparks, she grazed against the Breakwater and carried on out of the Eastern entrance - hotly pursued by the Admiralty tug, *Char*.

Conditions outside the harbour were terrible, but the gallant little tug managed to get alongside. Two officers and two ratings scrambled onboard the lifeless hulk. A tow rope was connected, but with the strength of the wind and tide little moved; apart from the *Montrose's* bitts, which buckled under the strain. As the *Char's* engine roared at full throttle, the inevitable happened. The hawser broke and the derelict *Montrose* drifted out of sight towards the dreaded Goodwins. The men onboard the doomed vessel knew their only hope of saving the ship, and themselves, was to drop her anchor, but they soon realised it had also been removed during her refit.

Meanwhile the lifeboat, *Charles Dibden,* had been unsuccessful in getting to the *South Goodwin lightship,* which had been driven past the Sands and into a minefield. Coxswain Adams felt it was prudent to anchor and await a moderation in the gale. The crew managed to squat down under the lee of the gunwales away from the cold spray, which was breaking over the bows of the boat. Their uneasy rest was soon to be disturbed. They watched in disbelief as the dark shape of the *Montrose* surged past them and bumped across the Goodwins. In the raging seas she went aground on the falling tide. Will Adams and his crew struggled to haul in their anchor and, with only a corner of the lifeboat's mizzen sail showing, they made for the wreck.

By the light of the full moon, the black hull of the liner could be seen through the surf. Incredibly some flares had been found by her meagre crew and ignited. Owing to the shoal water, and all the wires and nets hanging from the *Montrose's* sides, the lifeboat approached cautiously. The four men on board watched with apprehension as the *Charles Dibden* edged closer in the turmoil and as her anchor was let go, up-wind and tide, the lifeboat was veered towards the wreck. Two men on the *Montrose* jumped, as the small vessel scraped alongside the hulk, and managed to catch hold of the shrouds on the lifeboat's mast as they were helped into the rolling boat. However, this manoeuvre had been difficult and dangerous and so a rope was thrown to the remaining two seamen who, in turn, tied it to their waists and jumped into the surf. Speedily they were pulled towards the safety of their rescuers and, when aboard, they poured out their relief and thanks to the coxswain Adams. One of the survivors stated that it was the second time he had been saved from a shipwreck and expected not to be so lucky the third time. His premonition was to be realised quicker than he thought. Less than three weeks later their tug, the *Char*, would be in a collision four miles from the wreck, and every soul aboard would perish. It was also a strange coincidence that the last man who jumped from the ill-fated *Montrose's* deck on that stormy night was called Crippen.

***U-12's*** torpedo explodes on the starboard bow of H.M.S. ***Niger***

## *THE DAY WAR CAME TO DEAL*

For the uninitiated Deal is a sleepy old-fashioned town that lies between Ramsgate and Dover. To some it is quaint and traditional, but it also overlooks a very important safe haven and anchorage for ships in an area known as the Downs. The South and North Foreland give a lee from the wind in those directions and the Goodwin Sands breaks up the wave action from the east. In the past as many as 400 ships would be seen sheltering at anchor and it has been felt that the harbour that was built at Dover could have been better positioned and protected at Deal.

During the First World War the Downs were just as crowded with allied and neutral vessels. To make sure the neutral ships did not carry cargoes that could aid the enemy, a couple of patrol tugs would make the rounds, inspecting their manifests and consignments. In case of trouble or a refusal from a captain, H.M.S. *Niger*, a torpedo gunboat, was there to back up any arguments.

Since the beginning of the war, apart from the few times she had left her station to bunker and re-provision, the *Niger* had been anchored in the fairway, one and a quarter miles off Deal. Her silhouette was familiar to the local residents, but little did they know that on the 11th November, 1914, the vessel would disappear from their vision.

That fateful Wednesday started off sunny, with a freshening wind from the south that made the bright winter's morning quite mild. Although the war was in its third month, the promenading locals did not feel threatened as they took advantage of the weather. They watched the small Deal boats getting about their business ferrying pilots to and from the ships in the Downs.

One of those crafts was the small motorboat, *Elsie,* skippered by the Deal Lifeboat's second-coxswain, Harry Peason. As he conned his boat, three-quarters of a mile off Walmer Castle, he noticed a grey tube like object protruding perpendicular four feet above the surface. Thinking it was a piece of wreckage, he noted the area to enable him to pick it up on the way home. Little did he know this was the periscope of the *U-12*, and, as he explained later, he was that close he could have smashed it with a boat hook. In hindsight, had he taken that action he may have saved the Admiralty the loss of one of His Majesty's warships.

The *U-12* was not alone, she had a companion, the *U-11*, that was also stalking the *Niger* to the east; but owing to the anchored neutral shipping in her way she did not have a clear shot at her target.

On the *Niger's* bridge the officers of the watch had also seen the periscopes. The danger was realised that the ship had not generated enough head of steam to weigh her anchor in time. Commands were given for all the watertight doors to be secured. When the general order was sounded the majority of the 85 officers and crew were on the mess deck having their dinner.

Kapitanleutnant Walther Forstmann had taken advantage of the gentle neap tide and had no difficulty in lining up the *U-12' s* bow tubes. As he looked through the periscope he could see his victim tethered by her anchor. The freshening southerly wind was starting to fleck the wave tops with white as the ebb tide struggled against it. Just after noon he ordered only one torpedo to be fired, as he was so sure of his first kill; it would be the first of many throughout the conflict. With the lowering of the periscope, the small coastal submarine started to make her way back, unmolested, to her base at Zeebrugge.

In less than a minute the torpedo struck the *Niger*, a little beneath the fore-bridge, on her starboard side.

When the general order was given to close the watertight doors, the mystified sailors thought that a collision was about to happen. As some of them were rushing topsides to ascertain the situation, a violent explosion shook the ship fore and aft. The deck erupted throwing the seamen off balance and falling on top of each other and darkness and smoke engulfed the vessel as the ship's dynamos were demolished by the blast. Lieutenant Commander Muir was quick to muster his bewildered crew on to the deck of the warship.

***U-12*** leaving port

Suddenly the grim realties of war were brought home to the people of Deal and, as they watched, a column of black smoke was seen to rise from the *Niger,* followed by an explosion then by a second emission of smoke and steam, which arose and seemed to hang like a pall over the stricken vessel.
The Deal boats were the first at the scene to take off the warship's survivors, who had mustered at attention, on the gradually sloping deck, awaiting the order to abandon ship. In a disciplined manner, the sailors embarked on the small craft, filling them to capacity. The closing of the watertight doors had given the *Niger* an extra twenty minutes and, as the last men left, a petty officer noticed the white ensign was still flying from the *Niger's* stern. He ran aft, determined that it would not be the German foe that would lower the ship's flag as, wrapping the ensign about his body, he boarded one of the rescuing Deal vessels. As an act of defiance or patriotism, he then hoisted it on the mast of the gallant little beach boat. At 12:30 p.m. the *Niger* slowly went down by her head and rolled onto her starboard side, her masts bending under the strain as she glided under in eight fathoms of water.

A porthole from the ***Niger***

The main topic of conversation in the town that night was the *Niger* incident. Many of the boatmen were relating their version of the tragedy to the few residents who had not seen it happen. Was there a spy in the town? Some had seen flashing signal lights coming from a hotel on the seafront in the early hours of the morning. Others felt the presence of a large Dutch warship, that had passed through the Downs that morning, had brought the U-boats into the anchorage. Could there have been a German sympathizer in one of the neutral merchant ships who had radioed information to the awaiting U-boats? These were questions for which the answers were never known, although some eyewitnesses debated the disaster for many years later.

***Othello II*** before she became a minesweeper

## *DECKY LEARNER*

Just as dawn begrudgingly summoned another day, the boy cleared his throat and then spat out the contents into the muddy waters of Dover Harbour. As he leant against the guardrail of the armed trawler, he started to whistle the tune of a bawdy song he had heard the stokers singing the night before. He gazed out at the other trawlers and drifters moored nearby and noted that they all rolled in the choppy sea that even the confines of the breakwaters and piers could not subdue.

His thoughts took him back to the day the recruiting board had given him a position as ship's boy on the *Othello II*, recently from Hull. The dockyard workers had cleared most of her fishing equipment from the 110 foot vessel, and had installed different wire warps for mine sweeping and a gun on her foredeck. Her fishing number, H 956, and the Hellyer Steam Fishing Company emblem could just be made out under the new paint on her smoke stack. The 206-ton ship had only been in service for a couple of months and the skipper, with his crew of nine, were starting to work as a team on the daily patrol in the Channel.

By October 1915, life became too hectic for the boy to be homesick. Although his jobs were lowly ones, he was glad that he was part of that company, if only as a decky learner. His thoughts were interrupted by an angry shout from the engineer to 'stop his noise.' What was he trying to do, whistle up more wind than the gale that was blowing already? It had been a strong south-south east all night which had kept some of the fleet from their duties.

The *Othello* should have been out in those rough seas. It was only because the *Jackmar*, her companion minesweeper, had problems with part of her towing equipment they had not been able to sweep the shipping channel in the early hours. The crew had taken advantage of the unexpected Saturday night ashore and had spent most of their wages in the local pubs.

A message had been relayed to the trawler's skipper to cast off the mooring lines and make ready to leave the harbour, as the *Jackmar's* problems had been resolved. The report also informed that the Norwegian collier *Eidvisa* had struck a mine, and sunk just before 8 a.m. By now all the stokers' hangovers were forgotten in the heat and sweat, as they shovelled more coal into the open jaws of the fire grate to heat the boiler.

The night before, Oberleutnant Count von Schmettow, in the submarine *UC 6*, found it difficult to believe his luck that he was alone in the 'A' route channel, just off the South Foreland. He was puzzled, as normally there were pairs of armed sweepers scouring the shipping lane. He cautiously made the most of the inactivity and laid a close pattern of mines through the middle of the shipping's passage.

The German mine was different to the British version, as the lead tube horns concealed a glass cylinder full of battery acid. When a ship struck the mine, one of the horns, which stuck out from all over the weapon, was bent and the glass vial broken. The liquid fell into the battery making it active and detonating the explosive.

After Von Schmettow had sown his deadly cargo, he conned the *UC-6* back to the safety of Flanders.

As the *Othello* started to surge ahead in a heavy following seas, the crew felt and heard another explosion; the Clyde Shipping Companies' vessel *Toward* had hit another mine and was starting to sink bow first within a cable's length of the sunken *Eidsiva.*

When the trawler arrived in the area, they could see a group of drifters rescuing men from the sinking ship. In the middle of the melee was the armed steam yacht *Aries,* a fine 268 ton craft, that had been requisitioned by the Admiralty from the Duke of Leeds. She was in charge of the fleet of drifters and was trying to give orders by semaphore. There were other armed trawlers in the vicinity and some were trying to stop any more merchant ships from entering the restricted zone.

The crew of the *Othello* thought they saw a mine on the surface and started firing at it with their three pounder. The 'mine' turned out to be wreckage from one of the sunken ships. Meanwhile the *Aries* had ordered the drifters back to Dover and went about chasing a sighted mine inshore. As she approached the object an explosion blasted the vessel in half. When the smoke and debris cleared, there were dismembered dead lying on the sloping deck as the once elegant craft started to sink beneath the cold grey sea. Of the thirty-one crew only nine were saved.

In the mayhem, the naval craft realised they had been lured into a trap. The mines had

The ship-makers plate

been planted in positions that would sink the ships as they approached the original casualty to rescue the survivors. It would be less than half an hour before the next mine would claim another victim.

The *Othello* was ordered to continue to the north, towards Deal, and start to sweep at the beginning of 'A' channel. She had hardly made any way before another of the *UC 6's* deadly sown seeds viciously ripped her apart. In her wheelhouse were the skipper, a crew member, the helmsman and the decky learner. Before their dazed minds could take in what had happened, water started to enter the bridge and they knew that those below deck had not stood a chance. When the men tried to open the wheelhouse door, they found it had been distorted and firmly jammed shut by the explosion. As the water rose, the captain forced open the window, but the entrance was barely large enough for the boy to squeeze through. There was no time to argue as the men pushed the lad out of the window. His last sight of his shipmates was of them staring after him as the trawler slid beneath the waves.*

After a few days in the sickbay, the lad was posted to another Dover Patrol trawler, the *Weigelia.* His life took another turn for the worst as, within four months, this vessel was to also strike a mine, and sink less than two miles from his previous boat. Shortly after that, he was discharged from the Service for medical reasons. His young mind had been broken by his ordeals and by what his eyes had witnessed.

* It was because of this misfortune that all future Admiralty trawlers and drifters had their cabin doors removed and canvas screens put in their place.

A trawler's crew

## *TIP AND RUN*

Two hours before midnight on the 26th of October, 1916, twenty-four North Sea herring drifters tended their nets on a cold moonless night. Their dim shapes spread across the English Channel and it was only the occasional glow from a cigarette or pipe that indicated life on board. During the slack water, the monotonous chore of checking and mending nets had to be undertaken - in a few hours time their monotony would come to an abrupt end. The twenty-five miles of nets the drifters had set were certainly not for fish, they were made from thin galvanized wire with a mesh of ten to twelve feet, and their expected prey were U-boats.

Even with the submerged mine fields German submarines still managed to get through the Straits of Dover. Their aim was to attack or lay mines, which successfully sank shipping throughout the Allied sea routes. The Admiralty requisitioned drifters' nets did occasionally trap a submarine and, with the help of the destroyers that dropped depth charges around them, usually made a kill.

Although life for the sailors was hectic it could also be humdrum; defending the narrow

First turbine cross Channel passenger steamer ***The Queen***

stretch of water day and night was hard work, but the enemy was seldom sighted. There were full flotillas of monitors, destroyers, trawlers, transports and drifters at sea every day and night. It was only boiler cleaning and repairs that kept them in harbour for any length of time. The German ships, on the other hand, did not seem keen to fight, nevertheless their vessels were well maintained. Their hulls below the water-line were regularly careened, which gave them maximum speed and their crews were not stale from constant patrols.

Just before the high spring tide, which coincided with midnight, two divisions of German destroyers left the occupied port of Ostende. Using the extra depth of water they steamed over the anchored minefields. The mission of the twenty-four vessels was to search and destroy anything that got in their way. Their advantage would be surprise, and they knew that any ship that they encountered would be the enemy. As they skirted the Belgian shoals one of the divisions carried on along to the French coast and the other towards

Dover.

It was the old British destroyer, *Flirt*, which was the first to sight them. Unfortunately her officers made the fatal mistake of believing they were friendly vessels returning to the Downs, and let them pass unheeded. Within minutes gunfire was heard. The *Flirt* went to investigate and found a sinking drifter with her sailors in the water. The destroyer's captain lowered an officer and a rating into a boat to help rescue the survivors. It would be the last time they saw their destroyer - she was attacked and sunk by six of the German torpedo boat destroyers. After that, the enemy ripped through the drifters, whose only defence was a rifle and twenty rounds of ammunition. Seven were sunk and two more were badly damaged, along with an armed trawler.

A watch-keeper's bell from ***The Queen***

The other division of German destroyers steamed along the Boulogne-Folkestone route and came upon the 1,676 ton transport *The Queen*. She was unescorted, and luckily empty of troops. As shots were fired at the 300 foot ex-cross Channel ferry, she hastily hove to and the crew were quickly made to abandon ship. This was done in an orderly way and the only casualty was a cook, who had been badly scalded during the conflict.

*The Queen* was a fine ship; she had been built by Dennys of Dunbarton thirteen years previously for the South Eastern and Chatham Railway Company. Her job was to ply the lucrative short sea routes from Dover to France. Although the competition was great in those early days, her three propellers, driven by Parsons steam turbines, drove her at speeds of up to twenty knots, and she made the fastest crossings. It was because of her speed that she had been hired by the Admiralty as a troop carrier. Almost two years previously, to the day, she had gone alongside the French liner, *Admiral Gauteaume*, which had been torpedoed and was sinking. This act of bravery had saved the lives of two thousand Belgian refugees. King George V had personally congratulated Captain Carey of *The Queen* on this achievement.

As the German boarding party tramped along *The Queen's* deserted decks some set a fused bomb deep below her water line. The rest went in search for the ships papers and secret orders. The men quickly fulfilled their task and left - they would be her last passengers. The two German flotillas of destroyers re-grouped and they attacked and severely damaged another two British destroyers with torpedoes. After the ships lobbed a few rounds towards the shoreline of Dover, where two shells burst in the village of Hougham, they disappeared back to the Belgian port unscathed.

The charges on *The Queen* ignited, but possibly because the hole they had caused was not of a large enough size, or maybe because of the excellent construction of her bulkheads, she did not sink immediately. On the flood tide she drifted a distance of five miles from the Varne sandbanks, only to sink close to the South Sand Head, near the Goodwins.

This audacious raid had lasted only three hours, however, death and destruction lay in the wake of the German ships. Forty-five British officers and men were killed, four recovered wounded, and one officer and nine men were taken prisoners. Although the British fleet had done their best in the difficult situation of protecting the Channel, the Admiralty at London felt the whole affair had been handled badly. The Commander in Chief of the Dover Patrol, a practical but outspoken 'old salt', Vice Admiral Bacon, incited more wrath when he declared the raid as mere 'tip and run' and he remarked that he wanted to be left to get on with the job in hand. Unfortunately the Admiralty saw it differently, and after other disagreements, relieved him of his post before the war had ended; an act he would never forgive.

When local divers investigated the wreck in 1989, it was listed on the chart as an 'unknown'. Their first finds, on the almost intact vessel, were square shaped portholes - the type normally found on passenger ships. As there was no recorded vessel of that class in the area, they became puzzled. It was only when they found a small five and a half inch bell with *THE QUEEN* only just discernible on it, all was revealed. The main bell has never been found, perhaps the Germans took it as a souvenir of their success.

The telegraph salved from the wreck.

## *UNLUCKY U-BOAT*

On the 21st of November, 1917, the *U-48* started to nose out from the German port of Wilhemshaven. Kapitanleutnant Edeling was in the conning tower with his navigation officer. Their destination was to be the South coast of Ireland. It would be there that they could intercept and sink the American transports, full of troops and supplies, bound for Brest. They decided to take the shorter route through the Straits of Dover, as opposed to going the safe way, all around the British Isles. Although the narrow stretch of water was guarded by wire mesh nets strung across the Channel to ensnare the U-boats, many, by the darkness of night, had slipped over the top of them.

As the submarine edged past the moored up rows of her sister ships, the commander noticed that all their hatches were left wide open to the cold winter's air. The stench of human confinement for weeks in an enclosed space was hard to disperse. His vessel was of the ocean going type, with a maximum speed of 14 knots and a cruising range of 7,600 miles. Throughout the length of her 213 feet hull some of the engineers were ensuring that all of the machinery, in her cramped quarters, was in working order. As every available space was being used for provisions, those crew not on duty were confined to their bunks, to read books or newspapers.

What the news sheets did not tell them, but common knowledge to the sailors, was that the British blockade was having an effect on German food stocks. In May, the first outbreaks of discontent were being felt by the navy and three months later the German fleet actually mutinied. There was a crisis in morale and men were drafted into the submarine service against their will. Not only was their leave being rescinded, owing to the increased war effort, but also many of their comrades were not coming back from missions.

Even though the best food rations were reserved for the U-boat crews, and the incentive of higher pay was also offered to them, few new volunteers were attracted.

Two days out and sixty miles short of Dover the submarine was set upon by an aircraft. As she dived, the aeroplane dropped a bomb, which exploded very close to her submerged hull. The crew had looked at each other in fear; this was not a good omen so early in the voyage. By half past seven that night, she was on the surface heading at full speed to make the crossing of the nets beyond the *South Goodwin lightship*. However, a navigational mistake had been made, due to a compass fault, and her route was to be off course by ten miles. She strayed too far to the west and into the net barrage at the North Sand Head. As the nets fouled her propellers the oil-fired engines seized. Fortunately she had managed to sever the nets head-ropes with the bow cutter and the strands that

Deal boatmen pick over the remains of the ***U48***

remained fastened to her propellers became loose enough for her to gain headway by using her battery driven motors. As she started too proceed further, lost in the darkness, the crew felt an ominous bump and the *U-48* came to a halt.

Carl Edeling looked at the chronometer, 3 a.m. - and cursed his navigation officer. They were obviously on the Goodwin Sands and only a few miles away from the forces of the Dover Patrol. He tried putting the engines full astern to pull her off, but all he managed to do was to make a deeper furrow for the U-boat to lay in. It was only four hours to daybreak and the crew sensed the urgency in the order to lighten the ship. First to go was sixty tons of fuel oil and then most of the fresh water was pumped out; but she still did not move. Everybody mustered as the main hatches were opened on the pressure hull and three of the torpedoes, plus an amount of ammunition, were thrown overboard. It was only then that the U-boat started to stir as she lost the grip of the deadly sandbank.

As dawn broke the Admiralty drifters started to busy themselves to the routine of the day's work ahead. The smell of eggs and bacon wafted across Ramsgate Harbour on the cold November's breeze and within minutes a steady flotilla came out through the harbour entrance. The *Paramount* and *Majesty* started to couple up the hawser which kept them tethered together. As they paid out the wire to start the sweep, the skipper, with a steaming hot mug of tea in his hand, watched his crew of ex-fishermen. They performed smoothly and with experience. Their aim was to make sure the northern approach to the Downs was clear of mines. The drifters *Present Help*, *Acceptable* and *Feasible* were also there to perform similar duties.

The Dover based armed trawler *Meror* was the first vessel to sight the *U-48*, a mile from her starboard bow. In the first light of that morning, their gun crew rushed to action stations. The blast and recoil of the gun made the reinforced deck of the craft shudder. As the smoke cleared they saw that the drifters had also seen their prey.

They were hurriedly slipping their sweeps and making towards the enemy – their strategy would be to try and surround the submarine. Although the Admiralty paid a bounty of £1000 for any U-boat destroyed, it was pure courage that made the lightly armed drifters attack. They went in like a pack of hounds and a Maxim machine-gun was hastily mounted on to the wheelhouse roof of the *Paramount*. All of the drifters started to fire at the *U-48* with their small deck guns. At first the shells fell short, but they continued to close the range in the gradually shoaling waters.

Kapitanleutnant Edeling's worst nightmare was now coming true! They had, after all that work, only just freed the *U-48* and she was starting to motor to the southwest and into the deeper water. In front of him he saw a trawler racing down at full speed with her bow gun blazing. Abeam of him he could see the little fleet of drifters, in line abreast, getting closer. He blindly altered course and ended up, yet again, aground on the Goodwins.

The German ordered the gun crew to fire with their 4.1 inch and 22-pounder deck guns. The tired men knew they were fighting for their lives. Shells fell all around the fishing boats and the *Paramount* received a hit.

Just after 7 a.m. the old destroyer *Gipsy*, alerted by the gunfire, arrived on the scene. At 2000 yards, she opened up with a 12-pounder and then her 6-pounder; after the first four range finding shots, she hit the sub. In all, thirteen shells smashed into the *U-48* and her unprotected gun crews were raked by fire from the drifter's Maxim gun. Edeling knew he was beaten. As he destroyed the confidential books, he ordered some of his seamen to put short fused charges into the bow and stern torpedo tubes. Just before the explosions, twenty-two sailors jumped from the blood-stained deck of their dying craft. They were quickly picked up by a drifter's crew; the manoeuvre was made difficult as the wind freshened from the southwest.

Along with the prisoners, news of the engagement soon reached Dover, much to the delight of Vice-Admiral Bacon, the Commander-in-Chief of the Patrol. His salvage master, Captain Iron, wanted to see if he could reclaim anything of the wrecked vessel; but her position in the shallow water created a dilemma. He realised he needed local knowledge and commandeered the help of the Deal lifeboat, *Charles Dibden*. Along with the harbour tug, *Lady Crundall*, who stood near by, they managed, with difficulty, to get aboard the wreck. Inside the hull they discovered the carnage; the navigation officer had his brains blown out. It was rumoured that his captain was the culprit.

The following day a group of Deal boatmen went aboard her, to pick over the mangled remains. As they looked up they saw a lone figure, in a German uniform, watching them from the conning tower. Thinking he was a survivor from the action, they called out to him, only to see the man vanish. They quickly left the wreck and would never go near it again.

For years the *U-48* could be seen at most low tides on that desolate part of the Goodwins until it was eventually forgotten. However, it wasn't until 1973 that it was *re-discovered* by some Ramsgate divers. They started to strip her of the non ferrous metals concealed in the hull. The national newspapers got to hear about it and published a story of the U-boat just emerging from the sand. The barnacles and marine growth on the conning tower obviously proved this to be false. As the divers finished their summer's souvenir hunting they blew off the conning tower, which was partly made of brass, to be sold for scrap. This was the last time the unlucky U-boat would ever be seen above the sea again.

An armed trawler starts a dawn patrol in heavy seas.

The *Fearless of London*

## *FATE OF THE FEARLESS*

With a light southwest wind and foggy conditions the ketch *Fearless* slowly groped her way across the Channel. The cargo of two hundred tons of Belgian bricks made her low in the water. Even with all of her limp sails set the craft was hardly making headway and with the strong tide, she became difficult to handle. The vessels captain, Ernest Leek, had calculated that they would shortly sight the coast off Deal. As soon as their position could be verified, they would hug the land, down Channel, to their destination of Shoreham. On board were four of his seasoned crewmen along with his twelve year old son and a new decky learner. Joseph Sennet was eighteen years of age and this was his first ever voyage. As he peered through the mist, which had been with them all the way from Nieuwport, he considered whether he had made the right career decision. Even the skipper's young son, who had accompanied his father on many a voyage, seemed to know more about the sea than he did.

Tragedy nearly struck on that peaceful Sunday, the last day of September 1923. The white chalk cliffs of the South Foreland suddenly loomed up out of the mist. As the kelp covered rocks came into view Joseph shouted out the danger, but the helmsman had already seen it. The wheel was put hard over and everybody on deck waited with bated breath. The ketch was slow to answer. The shallow water and rocks almost seemed to reach out to the *Fearless*, amidships and then her stern. The vessel had gone about and the immediate danger was over.

Captain Leek decided to wait for more favourable conditions and steered his boat north towards the Downs. An hour later the anchor found a good hold a half-mile from the town of Deal.

In his cramped quarters Leek felt apprehensive. Four years previous, he had anchored off Deal in the barge *Corinthian*. It was there that he had a premonition of disaster and he sent his son ashore, to catch a train back to London, and home. Two days later, on the night of 2nd November, 1919, the *Corinthian* had foundered in a gale of wind a few miles from the Goodwin Sands. Captain Leek and his men had suffered an unforgettable nightmare. Of the crew of eight, only three were found clinging to the sunken vessel's rigging. They had been there for sixteen hours and when the lifeboat managed to pluck them to safety, one was found to be already dead. Even after a search there were no other survivors - he again sent his son ashore.

The *Fearless* had lain at anchor for four days. They watched the dropping barometer and black squally clouds from the north and saw the other vessels in the Downs up anchor and steam or sail to the south, to get a lee from the incoming storm. Ernest Leek knew it was time to continue his passage but first he needed some provisions. He and his crew rowed their small punt to Deal pier, to buy victuals from the town. Leek had left Joseph Sennet in charge of his craft. Within a few hours the tide had changed and with the ever freshening northwest wind the sea became quite lumpy.

As the small rowing boat was being thrown about like a cork it took a pounding against the pier. The captain of the ketch recognized that it was going to be difficult to get back to the *Fearless*. As the tide made, the sea got rougher. In their haste, one of the crew fell into the water and was saved from drowning by a couple of visiting pier anglers. Unfortunately in the confusion the vessel's punt had become so badly damaged, it had sunk.

Captain Leek was concerned that he could not leave his craft solely in command of a young lad. He hired a galley from the beach at North Deal, which managed to get him to his ship just before the force of the gale was unleashed.

Joseph Sennet helped him aboard. He explained to his captain that he was relieved to be released of his command. As he had watched, with apprehension, the waves getting higher, his only comfort had been the ship's cat - a mere kitten.

Throughout that night, great seas swept over the *Fearless* as she strained at her anchor. Captain Leek was regretting leaving his crew ashore. The ketch, already heavily laden and low in the water, was now getting lower. He tried manning the pumps but had to give up exhausted. Dawn was slow to break and the wind had not abated at all. By 9 a.m. the black squall clouds gave the illusion that, on this Thursday morning, daylight would not get any lighter than it was then.

It was a situation that the captain had been in before. With seas still breaking over her, the *Fearless* was a doomed ship and the water in her bilge was continuing to rise.

Within thirty minutes the Deal Lifeboat, *Charles Dibden,* was seen coming back from a rescue. Coxswain William Hoile saw the *Fairless's* signal of distress and attempted to put the lifeboat alongside the ketch. The manoeuvre was difficult and he knew that maybe only one chance would be had; with his local knowledge and seamanship it was done. Leek and Sennet thankfully scrambled aboard the seaworthy craft leaving the only living thing aboard the *Fearless*, the black kitten, mewing piteously in the scuppers.

The two survivors felt slightly better after a tot of rum and a good breakfast which was supplied by Mrs. Hoile, the coxswain's wife. John Prior, the local agent for the Shipwrecked Mariner's Society, cared for the rest of the crew. He and Leek renewed acquaintances.

From the pier and foreshore, many of the locals watched the derelict ketch taking a pounding. As she slowly dragged her anchor, at midday, her mainsail was torn away from their lashings. The wind and the ebb tide had driven the *Fearless* half a mile from her original anchorage on to a bank, east of Deal Pier. Just before 5:30 p.m. she went down stern first. She settled on the bottom with both her masts still visible and torn sails flaying in the wind. The following day the gale had abated, but the masts were still visible. There was much concern with the local fishermen. The wreck was in a position where they normally shot their herring nets and would have been a serious hazard to them. They petitioned Trinity House to disperse the wreck; which they did within a few weeks, but the 200 hundred tons of bricks remained on the sea-bed.

## *THE GULL COLLISION*

For the first three months of 1929 fog was a constant menace to shipping throughout the Downs. Some days in the light airs it was wispy, and others, in the words of the crew of the *Gull lightship* it was 'as thick as guts.' Fog when it's so dense that you cannot see the bows of your ship is unnerving. The thought of others navigating through the shipping lanes between the Goodwins would make even the most diligent men on watch see ghostly shapes of imaginary ships. In the first half of the twentieth century radar was not yet invented. Although caution and slow speeds were adhered to - collisions often happened. Most skippers would try to anchor up out of harm's way, until more favourable conditions prevailed. Lightships were placed in strategic positions to alert vessels of nearby hazards but, being tethered by a large anchor, could not alter course when impending danger bore down upon them.

The seven men crew of the *Gull lightship* always found some relief from their hardships below decks. The old wooden hull groaned with a familiar reassurance as the oil lamps cast shadows about the deck beams. The seamen's quarters were spotless, the brass fitments burnished bright and their dining table scrubbed white. Upon the stove, which was always alight, was a constant boiling kettle. Each one of the members of the crew supplied their own food for the two month stint on board. This, with a supplement of fresh caught fish, lasted them. Trinity House supplied the fuel and water.

The men, who were mostly ex-fishermen and sailors, got on together. Their ideals and beliefs were similar - it was only their choice of tobacco that differed as smoke from their pipes and cigarettes lingered below deck. The job was a constant one, as one watch finished, and the men climbed into their bunks, the next was on deck attending to their duties. As the mist became more intense the fog horn was pressurised by a hand pump, and, with the aid of the ship's chronometer, the signal was blasted out at regular intervals. The sleeping crewmen became used to the monotonous siren; although ear-plugs were issued, none bothered using them.

In the early hours of the 18th of March the watch, on the deck of the lightship, could hear the thumping of engines from a large steam ship. As they peered through the thick cold fog the massive bows of the 7,844 ton *City of York* loomed above them. Although she was

Repairing the lightship at Sandown Castle

The crew of the ***Gull light ship***

proceeding at slow speed the ship ploughed through the wooden hull. The crash of the light vessel's lantern breaking and the splintering of wood echoed through the darkness. As the *Gull* almost rolled over on her beam ends, she bounced off the liner's bow. Icy cold water rushed into the gaping hole, extinguishing the oil lamps and galley fire. The five men below, which included the captain, jumped from their hammocks, dazed. The large hole amidships extended below the waterline of the 103 feet vessel and she quickly started to settle lower in the water.

Although disorientated, the seamen's natural instinct of survival prevailed as they rushed topsides. They jumped into the sea as the lightship sank on an even keel. The two men on deck had managed to launch the ship's boat, which was already slung out on its davits, and rescued the men. In the swirling fog they searched in vain for their captain, David Williams.

When the Ellerman liner hit the small wooden vessel, the captain had promptly ordered her engines 'full astern' and then 'stop'. Without delay he picked up the lightship's crew from their lifeboat and provided them with hot drinks and dry clothes. At 4a.m. he alerted the authorities ashore, by wireless, of the disaster.

When the Ramsgate lifeboat arrived two hours later, they were surprised to find that two Deal boats were already there. They had steered a compass course to the wreck only to find the top of the lightship's mast and cage barely showing above the water. After a brief conversation with the master of the *City of York* to ascertain the safety of the light vessels crew, the boats departed from the scene.

Just after Harry Meakins boat, *Lady Beaty,* had returned from the wreck she was hired by Trinity House to act as an emergency lightship. When the 25 foot boat found her way back to the *Gull*, the six men tied a red flag on to the cage of the sunken vessel. By 8a.m. the small crew, equipped with a hand fog horn and a pocket watch, gave a regulation blast every two minutes. The fog thickened and visibility went down to six yards. Their pangs of hunger, from a missed breakfast, were soon forgotten when a couple of ships using the channel nearly ran into the *Lady Beaty*. By noon the fog lifted and several vessels, confused at not finding the *Gull* on station, started to wander to the east and close to the

Goodwins. The small boat's crew were kept busy by waving and shouting to prevent other accidents happening. Later that day the Trinity House steamer *Satellite* relieved the tired and hungry men from their vigilance .With relief they motored back to Deal beach.

Within weeks of a replacement lightship being positioned close to the wreck site, divers explored the sunken ship. As they felt their way about the *Gull*, in only a few inches of visibility, they came across the corpse of Captain Williams. They found him in a standing position, jammed against some woodwork. It was surmised that he must have arisen at the sound of the collision only to be trapped by the moving furniture in his cabin. As the ship sank, his death by drowning must have been horrific. The body was eventually removed from its wooden tomb and brought to the surface.

As the months went by, the Grimsby salvage company, Messer's Chalton and Co, were employed to salve the wreck. Their divers put wire strops around the sunken hull which were then attached to two lighters. To make the lighters sink several feet they were almost filled with water. The strops were tightened on the vessels at low tide and then the sea water was pumped out. As the tide rose so did the barges with their dead weight strung below them. At high tide the *Gull* was suspended 12 feet from the seabed and the lighters were towed shoreward until the wreck grounded. Every low and high tide the laborious routine was carried on, until the beginning of July when the ever shortening strops held the wreck of the *Gull* a mere 500 yards off the beach at North Deal.

On the 6th of July she was beached just north of Sandown Castle and crowds of solemn locals inspected the hull. She looked a sorry sight, with her iron fittings rusty and the raffle of the salvage men's warps on her deck. It took three days for the Grimsby firm to patch up the gaping hole in her side, and when finished, she was towed to a shipyard on the Tyne to be refitted. After the work had been completed, she was put back into service as the *Brake* light vessel. But she was never a popular berth for the lightship-men. Tales of a ghost walking below decks spread amongst the crews. Perhaps it was the lost spirit of the captain, trying to find his way out of the sinking vessel.

Crewmen deemed her as an haunted

The remains of the ***Aragonite*** were a danger to shipping

## *TOWING KING GEORGE'S TRAWL*

Under the cover of thick fog, four German destroyers slipped out of port trying to keep sight of each other. In command of the small flotilla was Kapitan Bonte. As the vessels *Wilhelm Heidkamp*, *Hans Ludemann*, *Karl Galster* and *Hermann Kunne* proceeded cautiously across the Channel they could hardly believe their luck at not being challenged by the British. Although the Second World War was in its second month most of the shipping that night had come to a halt and was anchored up - hopefully out of the way of the foolhardy. In the swirling mist the Germans laid a lethal pattern of 288 mines in the approaches of the Thames Estuary. Within hours the British destroyer *Blanche* was sunk and the mine laying cruiser *Adventure* was badly damaged. The cargo ships *Matra* and *Ponzano* were also destroyed, along with the *Woodtown* the following day.

Although the mine was a British invention, and had proved its worth in the previous war, the Germans had perfected a new version - the deadly magnetic mine. At the outbreak of hostilities the German Navy mobilized as many of their U-boats, that they had available, to plant mines in the convoy routes of the English Channel. To combat this menace trawlers were hired for anti-submarine and mine sweeping duties. They also helped to lay mine barrages across the U-boats bolt holes which were through the sand banks of the Nore and Goodwins. The *U-12*, *U-40* and *U-16* were the first to fall victims to the British subterfuge. It was because of the Royal Navy's successes that the enemy decided not to risk any more valuable submarines in the narrow straits - yet mines still had to be laid.

The four years old, 315 ton, trawler, *Aragonite*, had been busy since she had been commissioned two months earlier at the outbreak of war. There was a faint smell of fish about the Hull vessel and she still had the Kingston Steam Trawling Company crest on her smoke stack. The crew wondered when she would be docked to get her grey paint, and anything else the Admiralty would install to make her a ship of war. Life aboard her was not quite as relaxed as the good old days when she was earning a living catching cod from the North Sea. The skipper did not wear a cloth cap or talk with a Suffolk drawl as did most of the crew. He had a smart uniform with a gold wavy stripe on his sleeve and his voice had an educated clip to it. Although most of the crew were fishermen they put up with the 'old man's' moans about the slackness of things aboard. He explained that Britain was at war and the pressure was on. From the skipper downwards they would all be learning. However, because of the fatal danger of too many mistakes the crew must start to become an able body of seamen and get into the routine of running a ship in His Majesty's Navy.

On the 18th November, 1939, another flotilla of German destroyers put to sea - again under the cover of more fog. In the early hours they laid a mine field through the approaches to the Dover Straits. Casualties were soon to fall prey to the new menace and every available mine-sweeper was sent out to clear a safe channel for the allied merchantmen to get through.

As HMS *Aragonite* 'was pulling her weight' and sweeps, mines were being released from their moorings and blown up by concentrated rifle fire. Although much was routine, each one of the seventeen crewmen had a job to do; be it keeping a look out for aircraft or making sure the galley fire was always alight for a well earned cuppa. By the 22nd November the *Aragonite* had been at sea for three days, the men were tired. She was now slipping back to Dover for refuelling and to take a few hours break from the tension. When she approached Deal the sailors noticed much allied and neutral shipping anchored in the Downs, awaiting inspection from the Naval Contraband Patrol.

It was just outside the anchorage that a massive upward thrust almost lifted the trawler out of the water as a mine exploded under her hull.

As the pillar of water from the explosion had risen to a height of thirty feet the deck was awash. There were great volumes of smoke and steam coming from her holds. The crew was dazed and four were seriously injured with broken legs. Through the chaos, some semblance of discipline was resumed and acts of heroism were carried out; which were later to be rewarded by medals from the King. A damage report confirmed that the trawler was becoming un-seaworthy and the men got ready to abandon ship. The wounded were carefully brought on to the deck, topsides

Two patrol tugs raced to the crippled trawler and managed to take off all of her survivors. They knew the only hope of saving the *Aragonite* was for the craft to be towed the short distance to be beached. Thick hawsers were attached to her bitts and the tugs took up the slack. As the craft were straining at their task, the gradually sinking vessel started to bump the sea bed. She settled half a mile from the beach opposite the ruins of Sandown Castle. It was confirmed that nothing else could be done, and both of the tugs had to cast off their now dead tow and return the casualties ashore.

The wreck was to be a reminder of the deadly mine warfare and her masts were a familiar site throughout the war years. Many a skipper cursed them on a black night as they conned their craft through the Downs. In the early months of the war many lessons were learnt the hard way. Eventually the Straits of Dover were secured and made safe for the many thousands of ships that passed through them - thanks mainly to those gallant men in their converted trawlers towing King George's trawl.

Shortly after the war, the Navy cleared up most of the visible reminders of the past hostilities and the *Aragonite's* mast and superstructure were soon levelled. Being so close to the small ships anchorage Trinity House positioned a large, can shaped, green wreck buoy alongside her remains, much to the annoyance of the local herring drift netters. It was eventually removed in the late 1960s.

It was an unusual noise, but one that would become familiar to the crew of the lightship. The sound was not unlike a chain being swept at speed against the ship's hull. It was the shock wave of an exploding magnetic mine. Through the 'clag', which the cold easterly wind had produced, the deck-watch on the North Goodwin light vessel looked towards a south bound convoy of ships. With their hands buried deep into their duffle coat pockets, on that wintry afternoon of the 9th of January, 1940, they saw a column of water envelop the largest ship in the convoy. It was followed by a dull rumble as her foremast toppled. As she started to sink bow first the Trinity House sailors turned away from the grim scene; there was nothing they could do, Hitler had claimed another victim from Churchill's Armada.

The Union Castle liner, *Dunbar Castle*, had been dealt a death blow. The mine had exploded below the bridge, on her starboard side. As the steel foremast crashed down onto the bridge, where Captain Causton had been standing, he was fatally injured. The force of the explosion had also thrown the second officer from his bunk and against the deck-head, which fractured his right leg.

Lunch had just been served to the forty-eight passengers, some of whom were evacuees trying to escape the war. A number of the crew were also finishing their meal as the upward thrust of the detonation jarred the hot fat from the pans and on to the paraffin-fired stoves. The galley erupted in a mass of flames which engulfed the head waiter and five of his staff. Through the stench of burning fat and flesh they strove to put out the fire.

The chief officer, Herbert Robinson, took control, he, together with seaman Akehurst, quickly went below decks to search for the injured. The smoke filled area was in turmoil, with many of the passengers hurriedly attempting to get their possessions together.

10,002 ton ***Dunbar Castle***

Robinson informed the engineers to shut down the oil-fired engines and abandon ship. Feeling the ship start to slope forward he returned top-sides and they found the boat decks were nearly awash. The dazed but disciplined crew were already launching the lifeboats in an orderly fashion. Some of the stewardesses were tending to the wounded, and comforting the passengers, as they donned their kapoc filled lifejackets.

The escort minesweepers were scuttling around the dying ship; but also ever alert for a U-boat, which they suspected had destroyed the *Dunbar Castle*. The coaster *Loanda* broke convoy to help the survivors. As the lifeboats left the stricken vessel the last person to leave was the radio officer. Gradually the broken-backed liner settled upon the sea-bed, with only her bridge, funnels and mast showing above the water. The little flotilla of lifeboats headed for Deal, twelve miles away. As they approached the pier the urgent and continuous sound of the accompanying *Loanda's* steam whistle alerted those ashore.

Before the coaster had dropped her anchor the longshoremen had launched their boats and brought the survivors to the beach. The ARP, St Johns Ambulance Brigade along with the doctors and nurses from the local hospital awaited the casualties. Those that had been burnt were in a sorry state, covered from head to foot in blisters and in great pain. Swiftly they were transferred to Deal hospital in the care of Dr Hall.

In a near by café the unhurt survivors were given hot drinks and cigarettes. As they morosely huddled around the tables they were surprised to hear the sound of a popular tune being played from a piano. The melody came from the *Dunbar Castle's* musician who had found a piano in the corner of the restaurant. Within minutes some normality was brought back into their lives - they were thankful to be alive. In all, nine people were lost from the sinking, however, if it had happened further out to sea they realised their predicament would have been a lot worse.

The hulk of the *Dunbar Castle* remained in her semi-sunk state. As the days went by much of the 4,400 tons of general cargo was washed out of her holds. Also included in the flotsam were cabin trunks, cabinets and solid mahogany saloon chairs, from the liner's state rooms. These were viewed with interest by the crew of the *North Goodwin Lightship*, but most of the best finds just floated out of the reach of their boat hook. The wreck became the largest ship ever to be sunk in the proximity of the Downs and throughout the war years she stood as a constant memory to an unseen danger lurking below the waves.

The magnetic mine menace was soon to be dealt with, after a five foot dome-ended monster was inadvertently dropped by parachute on to the sands at Shoeburyness. Bomb disposal officer Lieutenant-Commander Ouvry had the dubious task of making it safe. As he cautiously dismantled the mine he was startled to find that it had more than one detonator. Although it seemed like a lifetime, Ouvry completed the job by 4:40p.m. on that same day - he had discovered the secret of Germany's latest weapon.

It was because the mines sat on the seabed that the minesweeper's wire could not to disturb them; but a steel ship's magnetic field would be enough to detonate the massive amount of explosive. It was also realised that they were being dropped at night by aircraft. The ARP set up listening and watching patrols along the sea fronts of the south-east coast. To detonate these mines, wooden Admiralty drifters towed skids with coils of copper wire. The coils were made live by passing a current through it from batteries. Aircraft flew low over the shipping lane armed with a magnetic coil strapped to their fuselages. Their passes were swift as the pilots knew that the water spouts from an exploding mine could take their tailplane off. All these methods gave reasonable results but it wasn't until the minesweepers were fitted with LL sweeps and the ships themselves were de-gaussed that the magnetic mine hazard was conquered.

# *THE PIG'S NAME WAS ADOLF*

At the outbreak of the Second World War the Downs was sealed off by the Naval Contraband Control. With guard ships stationed at each end of the anchorage all vessels of every nationality were incarcerated. Foreign ships were thoroughly searched, papers checked and the crew list inspected for spies, or cargoes which could help the enemy. With the constant shipping using the Channel the anchorage became very busy. For some ships, it would take weeks before they could be cleared by the naval officers.

Within the first six months of the war the Germans had sunk over two million tons of allied shipping, mainly by U-boats and the new magnetic mine. Neutral craft that were still plying a trade had their nationality painted on the hulls in bold letters, to deter mistaken identity and attack.

One such neutral was the Belgian steam ship *Flandres*, a thirty-two year old 422 feet long cargo vessel. She was up-anchoring after receiving her clearing papers from the Downs Control Base. The master and crew had patiently waited in the crowded anchorage for days. It was not a captain's favourite place to be, on that cold February of 1940. The stormy seas were often breaking away moored mines, both the enemies and British, which drifted in the tide. As the 5,827 ton vessel from Antwerp slowly manoeuvred through the cluster of waiting ships to continue her voyage to Montevideo, another Belgian ship collided with her.

The *Kabalo* ripped into the *Flandres*, portside amidships, smashing some of the lifeboats to pieces, toppling the wireless mast and severely crippling her. For a time the two ships

The Belgian steam ship ***Flandres***

were locked together, and as the *Kabalo* swung off, she ripped out more steel plates from the *Flandres* hull, enlarging the hole.

A tug, that was near-by, secured a tow line on the sinking casualty and started to pull her towards the shore. The 45 crewmen abandoned ship in the remaining seaworthy life-boats. However, the tug's task was futile; with the gash below the waterline sea filled the laden holds. As she started to go down the Walmer lifeboat quickly arrived on the scene.

The Captain, Chief Officer and a couple of engineers were the last to leave the strickened vessel and boarded the *Charles Dibden* just in time. The wreck sank on an even keel in sixty feet of water - and it was then that her hatches started to burst open. Large baulks of timber and cases of the cargo were shot to the surface, putting the lifeboats at risk of being holed. Seeing the danger, the coxswain of the local boat towed the other two full ships' lifeboats ashore. The cold grey sea enveloped the *Flandres* and only her stern mast and funnel could be seen, the two miles, from the beach, opposite Deal Castle.

Half an hour later, a patrol vessel checking out the area spotted an object swimming in circles around the wreck. As the boat approached it, they were amazed to find the swimmer to be a very bewildered pig, which was duly rescued. When the porker was handed over to the authorities ashore it was found out that its name was Adolf and it had been a temporary pet aboard the *Flandres*. The fate of the pig is unknown - but it never made quarantine.

Within months Germany's armies over-ran Europe. The once busy Contraband Control anchorage started to thin out as the neutral ships sailed back to home ports that had not been overrun by the enemy. After Dunkirk, the Germans installed large cross-channel guns which quickly found the range of the allied shipping. With the enemy's command of accuracy on inert objects in the Dover Straits, the Contraband Control was abandoned. Throughout that hot calm summer of 1940 the Downs was devoid of anchored ships. Only the wrecks remained visible, which were used as target practise for Spitfires, Hurricanes and MTB's.

During the war years the hulks that littered the Channel were a constant threat to the convoys. Two ships, the *Fluor* and *Brier* did run up on the wreck of the *Flandres* but were lucky enough to escape her clutches at high tide. As peace came to Britain it was realised the dangers had to be removed, for the safety of shipping, and the Navy set to the task. In November, 1946, H.M.S *Lundy* was in charge of demolition. The crew aboard the ship's cutter laid ten depth-charges in the Belgian wreck. As they paid out the wire, which was connected to the detonators, the negative end shorted out on the wet deck. The sea erupted and the small boat was blown to pieces. Incredibly, of the seven men in the launch, four were rescued barely alive, and were rushed to the Royal Marine's infirmary at Walmer. Within hours one more died. The *Flandres* was almost completely flattened with not much more than twenty feet of twisted steel left protruding from the sea-bed over a vast area. So ended the life of the ship, which is now home to numerous pouting and the occasional cod.

On the wreck of the ***Flandres***

***James Harrod*** ablaze in the Downs

## *DUTCH COURAGE*

From the stern rail of the 500 ton Dutch ship *Tromp*, Captain Harman Heida surveyed the many large vessels anchored in the Downs. It was just two weeks into the year of 1945 and the war in Europe was nearly over. Since the D-Day landings, the British and their Allies had swept through the occupied countries and were on the doorstep of the aggressor. The Canadian 8th Infantry had captured the large shore guns, which had kept the Downs empty since the capitulation of France in 1940. Now, free from any bombardment, the anchorage was full again.

Most of the vessels, awaiting orders and convoys, were 7,000 ton Libertys, full of supplies for the advancing troops. The American-made Liberty ship was an emergency product, with different parts coming from as many as twenty separate companies, and then put together at shipyards throughout the U.S.A. To make a saving in time, and 600 tons in weight, the pieces were wielded instead of riveted - and this meant that 43 miles of weld went into every ship. Because of the shortage of cargo ships, speed of construction was essential and the vessels were manufactured in weeks. One shipyard boasted that the keel of the next ship would be laid before the previous one had hit the water on being launched. All of the Libertys were named after dead eminent Americans and sailors.

With dusk, the south-westerly wind freshened and the dark murky waters in the Downs became lively. As Captain Heida completed his rounds of the ship, he made sure that his anchor light was bright and visible and he also released a little more chain; with the close proximity of the other moored up ships, this was not a safe area in which to drag anchor. At 10 p.m. he turned in, leaving orders to the seamen on-watch to keep a good lookout and awaken him if any of the other vessels looked as if they were getting too close. The wind by now had nearly reached gale force.

It was a loud explosion that had awoken him in the early hours. When Heida had jumped out of his bunk he was already dressed, which was the way seamen slept in those dark days of war. He quickly added a jumper and a duffle coat to stave off the cold January air. As he reached the deck he had no need to speculate on the disaster, the anchorage had been lit up by a burning ship.

Close by, he observed the Liberty ship *James Harrod* had collided with an anchored sister ship the *Raymond B Stevens*. The impact had caused part of the *James Harrod's* cargo of petrol to ignite and explode, instantly killing five sailors. The roar of the flames and detonation of the full gasoline cans were deafening. As the fire spread through the ship the Liberty's crew, justifiably, panicked and made to abandon her. Amongst the disorder and confusion some of the officers and men had gone forward and managed to release her anchor - a blazing ship drifting through a crowded anchorage would have brought chaos and destruction.

Captain Heida watched in disbelief as no other ship made any attempt to go to the assistance of the casualty. His own ship had just unloaded a cargo of petrol at Ostende and was a potential fire risk, yet he had no hesitation in ordering his men to up anchor. All of his sailors had mustered on deck at the noise of the blast, but a few of them were reluctant to carry out their skippers command. Some of the crew disputed the order and stated that it was madness to go anywhere near the inferno. They tried to reason with their skipper that they had come through the war years unscathed, and now did not want to be put in mortal danger from this allied victim.

The Dutch captain's attitude was resolute and could not be persuaded to differ. When a crewman's nerve broke, he made a lunge at Hieda. As the master sidestepped the panic stricken seaman, he hit the decky on the head with the binoculars that he was holding in his hand. It was only the sailor's cap peak that saved him from having a split skull as he staggered away dazed. With the raging fire not only illuminating the vessel's deck, but also the low clouds off Deal, the incident was seen by his men. Within minutes they started to carry out their work with haste.

Heida conned his ship to the bow of the *James Harrod*, where the last of her crew had some respite from the heat and flames. As the *Tromp* brushed the side of the towering bow, the panicking Americans poured over the guard rails of their ship. As they jumped on to the small ship's deck below, it was a miracle that some of them did not break their legs. Fortunately the manoeuvre had taken long enough for the remaining ten men to be saved and the captain then called for full ahead to clear the other vessel's anchor chain. One of the last men to come off the Liberty ship was her captain - who had been struck dumb with shock.

As the *Tromp* pulled away from the floating inferno, cans of flaming petrol cascaded into the night sky.

The American seaman hugged Heida and shook his hand vigorously. One man's relief at being rescued was so great that he offered to take the master to the States and give him all of his money. Hieda politely refused; after the war he would receive his reward with a document granting him the freedom of America from the Secretary of State and a decoration from his own Queen, Juliana of Holland.

At daybreak, the *James Harrod* was still ablaze and went on burning for six days, defying the gallant attempts from the National Fire Service, in their especially equipped boats, to douse the flames. Another severe gale from the southwest arose with the wind at times reaching 80 m.p.h. It was lucky for the residents of Deal and Walmer that the storm blew the smoke offshore, as it would have choked the town if the wind direction had shifted to the east.

Tugs eventually beached the burnt-out ship at Kingsdown, but she re-floated and drifted north with the flood tide, until finally grounding on the Malms rocks opposite Deal Castle. On the 22nd of January, as the blackened hull cooled and with her 441 feet hull beached in the shallow water, she started to split in half. She became a total wreck - although it could be seen that some of her cargo was salvageable.

Landing craft spent the following months alongside her, offloading trucks and 4 gallon cans of petrol. The sea around the ship had a multicoloured sheen from the spilt fuel, which would drift on the tide for miles. The petrol was then taken by lorry to a camp just outside of Deal for examination. The non-contaminated cans were driven to Walmer railway station and poured into a railway tanker.

On the 12th of September, just as their day's work was nearly over, five more men died. Perhaps it was a sneaked cigarette or a spark from a soldier's boot that caused the catastrophe. The vapour from the empty cans had ignited in a fireball and the soldiers from the US Labor Corps died a horrible death.

When all the salvageable cargo had been removed, the fore-part of the ship, which was now in two halves, was towed away to the River Blackwater. In 1946, that part of the crippled three year old vessel was loaded with obsolete chemical ammunition, towed out and scuttled in the North Sea. For many years the after-part of the *James Harrod* remained a prominent feature just off the foreshore, and was a popular diving platform for the local youths in the summer months. The eventual demolition of the eyesore was left to a brass helmeted diver, called Larry Parks, who removed her plate by plate and left hardly enough scrap in the twenty feet of water to harbour a few lobsters.

The hull started to split in half

Part of the ship grounded in Sandwich Bay

## *ONLY THE GOODWINS TAKES LIBERTYS*

Sixteen-year-old David Aggett was employed by Frederick Upton, coxswain of the Walmer lifeboat. His job was as a beach-hand to Upton's two motor boats on Walmer beach. He also occasionally assisted him, when he went afloat, to the ships that were anchored in the Downs. Although the Second World War was over, there would still be as many as fifty merchant ships in the anchorage. They would be there waiting to receive orders, from a Royal Naval officer, of their routes through the un-cleared minefields.

These ships had many requirements, sometimes provisions, and sometimes the services of James Hall, the famous lifeboat doctor, who suddenly found himself involved with attending to sick seamen. David knew he was only a small part of that illustrious team of fearless men, but he was proud to be there and was enthralled with their commitment. Joe Mercer, the old former lifeboat coxswain, who had turned seventy, was his mentor and taught him a great deal about the sea. When the lad had assured him that he could do a job, which then went wrong, Joe would say "That's the trouble with you young un's, you don't know narthing and carn't be told".

Due to the congested conditions, caused by the continual arrival of shipping in the Downs, accidents often occurred which required the launching of the Walmer Lifeboat. As David was too young, he could not go on her - Freddie always refused his pleas to be allowed to join the crew. Part of his job as 'beach boy' was to observe the ships coming into the Downs from the direction of Dover, south of Deal. The high chalk cliff of St

Margaret's Bay was at a juncture that the ships used to appear. Immediately they began to show he would espy which ship she was, where she was bound, and if she required a pilot or not. These signs he could read from her International Code flags; which, he had become expert in deciphering. If the ship did request a pilot, he would run to the Alma public house, adjacent to Walmer Green and opposite Freddie's white beach hut, to fetch him and his soul mates - the pilot would often enough be there as well.

On the 12th of September, 1946, he was left in charge of the deserted beach. It was a beautiful sunny day with no wind and a flat calm sea. His 'boss', along with his cohorts, were all in the Alma. Around midday, David gazed out to sea and spied a Liberty ship emerging from around the cliffs off the South Foreland lighthouse. He went into Freddie's hut and picked up the large leather covered telescope from its brackets over the stable type door.

The ship was unusually far out, and her national flag was indistinguishable. He also noted that she did not fly any other flags of command. The lad realised that the captain had not picked up a pilot, at Dungeness, as she was making for the *South Goodwin lightship*. Just before the vessel approached the light float she turned to port and steamed down the west side of the sand bank. Her progress was slow and tentative, and David was in no doubt that she was lost.

By now Freddie and his friends were in attendance, and the telescope was passing from one boatman to another. A discussion ensured whether to launch Fred's boat, *Rose Marie*, so that they could put him or Joe aboard and bring the vessel into the Downs anchorage. As the large ship was so far out, their thoughts were that on her present course, she would run on to the sands, to the north of Trinity Bay. Within seconds the situation was taken out of their hands.

Suddenly the North Deal Coast Guard fired two red maroon-rockets, their flares gracefully arching the blue sky. The message was 'You are standing into danger', and the vessel immediately responded by turning to port - instead of stopping her engines to consider the implication of her predicament.

All of these actions seemed, to those ashore, to be happening in slow motion. The vessel suddenly stopped as she ran up on to the Goodwin Sands.

Freddie, Lardie Dadd, Frenchy Baker and others all rushed towards Walmer Lifeboat Station, closely followed by young David - who did not want to miss out on this momentous occasion. Once there, the boatmen available struggled to put on their reddish brown life jackets, which hung on large pegs just inside the lifeboat-house door. The young boy was ordered to go to the bell rope and ring the boathouse bell, which was housed on the upper part of the building. What with the bell clanging away and the maroons having already exploded, it was not long before many helpers arrived to launch the lifeboat. Those men pulled large greased woods down the shingle beach by their rope lanyards and positioned them in the path of the reserve *Langham* lifeboat.

Percy Cavell, the lifeboat's engineer, appeared with other members of the crew and once on board, the slip chain was knocked open with a hammer, which unleashed the lifeboat. She slid quickly and easily over the woods, gathering speed as she passed down the sloping beach. In an impressive cascade of water, which splashed high either side of the craft's bows she sliced into a perfectly calm sea. Whilst the lifeboat was on its way to the stranded vessel, David went with the other boatmen to launch the *Rose Marie*.

Once the *Langham* lifeboat was alongside the stricken vessel they could see that she was the 7,000-ton Liberty ship, *Helena Modjeska*, of the Black Diamond Line. The ship had sailed from Marseilles and was loaded below and above deck with stores and army vehicles, which were to be discharged at Bremerhaven. Freddie went aboard to discuss the ship's future and the urgent need to get a kedge anchor out to assist warping her off the Sands. The captain commanded him to get off his ship, saying that she would re-float herself at high tide. Freddie returned to the lifeboat and continued to stand by alongside. Again he climbed the rope ladder, hanging from the ship's hull, to try to reason with the captain; again without success.

High water came and went. The *Helena Modjeska* shuddered, as her engine was put into astern. Great fountains of water emerged from the single propeller as it flailed around and churned the sea and sand in vain hope to break her free. The master knew nothing of the powers of the Goodwin Sands and by now it was too late to lay out that vital kedge anchor.

The captain had been warned by a man with many years of local experience, assisting ships that had been in the same predicament as the *Helena Modjeska.* As the tide fell, it became evident to the captain that he had lost his ship. The crew were being taken ashore by the lifeboat when six tugs arrived to attempt to pull her off the sands. Their labours were also ineffective and their efforts were to break the 440 foot, two year's old welded hull in half.

In the next few weeks, a great effort was put into salvaging the two halves. Her deck cargoes of military vehicles for the American forces in Germany and stores from inside the stranded vessel were discharged with difficulty. The after section of the hull was re-floated, and then beached at Sandwich Bay and the fore part was moored off Deal. Eventually both halves of the hull were towed to the River Blackwater and sold for scrap.

The only real casualty of the wreck was her master, Captain William Henry Curran, who, two days after her stranding, was found dead in a Ramsgate hotel. His guilt of the loss should have been equally born by the American Administration for Ship Operators; whose directive stated 'Many cases have been observed where pilots have been employed by ship masters at great expense and without authority, for waters such as the English Channel, North Sea and Baltic. Employment of pilots in such waters is considered unnecessary as the subject waters are of wide expanse and relatively free of danger. The employment of pilots in these waters is therefore disapproved.' Many of the American charts did not show the Goodwin Sands as a danger and some did not even include the lightships that surrounded them. In the same year of 1946 a total of three Libertys went aground on the Sands, only one surviving. The following year the American Administration rescinded their cavalier instructions.

Walmer Lifeboat

## *CALAMITY CORNER*

The gallant crew of the Walmer Lifeboat felt slightly uncomfortable in the plush surroundings of the Royal Hotel. Although this Deal hotel was frequented by Nelson in the past, it was not the normal drinking establishment of these men. They were there to be honoured by the French Consul-General.

Monsieur Gauther said in faulting English "Thanks to you thirty eight of my compatriots are still alive, and so French sailors are still happy and peaceful. I do not think I can say more in praise for the rescuers."

All those who attended that meeting were in the same frame of mind as once again the lifeboat had safely plucked lives from the dreaded Goodwin Sands. After a few drinks the crew started to relax and enjoy the glowing fire and comforts of the leather armchairs. It was then that their thoughts drifted back to the horrific night, three weeks before.

Black rain clouds had brought darkness an hour early on Sunday 13th January, 1952, and the townspeople of Deal and Walmer were soon to realise that this was going to be the worst gale they had witnessed all winter. Slates started to fly off roofs as the wind suddenly reached storm force and the torrential rain stained many a ceiling.

Quite a few prayers were said by those who heard the sound of the maroons explode just after 11 o'clock. As the crew ran to man Walmer Lifeboat they merely shrugged off the elements and cursed the weather. Whilst the beach crew got the launching woods ready, the coastguards explained to the waiting coxswain that a ship was reported aground on the Goodwins, near the South Sand Head. In the darkness, the lifeboat was quickly lost from sight as it plunged down the beach and into the rough sea.

As Coxswain Freddy Upton conned the lifeboat towards the *South Goodwin lightship* he

Remains of the ***Agen***

wondered why he could not see the casualty's deck lights.
He searched the inside edge of the sands, but with the freezing driving rain squalls, his men were finding it difficult to peer through the obscurity. Suddenly they spotted the faint red glimmer of a flare on the seaward side of the Goodwin Sands. The coxswain put the wheel hard over and tried to steam directly across the sands. Before he got halfway he found the seas so huge in the shallow water that he had to go about before his own craft became yet another statistic of the Goodwins.
After going the long way around the massive sandbank, and being at sea for nearly five hours, he finally found the French steamer, *Agen.* He realised the reason for the lack of radio information and lights; the 4,186 ton La Rochelle registered ship had broken in two.
In mountainous seas he tried, fourteen times, to put the lifeboat alongside the bow section of the freighter. It was where 38 of her crew were huddled, trying to get protection from the tremendous waves that were breaking over the two halves of the wreck. Although Freddie Upton did not want to give up he recognized the danger, and not wishing to be swept on to the deck of the casualty, had to stand off until six the next morning. By this time the tide and sea had moderated slightly and he steamed the lifeboat between the two jagged sections, which were only thirty feet apart. Cork and rope fenders were put against the hull, to stop too much damage from occurring, as the *Charles Dibden,* nudged up against the strickened ship. As the small boat surged up and down the hulk's side they started to rescue the crew. They slid down a rope and were physically man-handled aboard the tossing lifeboat by the seat of their pants and coats. Only the captain of the *Agen* remained onboard the wreck. Again and again the lifeboat coxswain pleaded with the captain to abandon his vessel - but he stubbornly refused. He could hardly believe that his journey from Dakaar should end like this, so near to his port of destination, Hamburg.
With the lifeboat low on fuel, one of the French crew hurt with a back injury and the rest suffering from exposure, Coxswain Upton reluctantly made his way back ashore. By 8 a.m. he had landed the steamer's crew, refuelled the lifeboat, snatched some spare cans of petrol and had returned to the shipwreck with its sole inhabitant. As the lifeboat came alongside, Captain Maurice Landreau perceived the impossibility of the situation. His deck cargo of 300 mahogany logs, many weighing over three tons apiece, was shifting. The cabin cruiser which had been lashed aft, had been smashed to pieces and the cotton and coffee cargo stowed in the holds was spoilt. His ship had also broken in two, completely unsalvageable.
It was just before eleven that morning when the lifeboat was winched up the beach and released her remaining survivor from the wreck. The lifeboat crew, after hot drinks, flopped into their beds to get some well deserved sleep.
Some hours later on Monday afternoon, frantic radio messages were being sent to Dover Coastguard. Puzzled skippers of ships and trawlers had found that huge baulks of timber were floating around in the very busy shipping lanes of the Dover Straits. The Trinity House vessel *Ready*, with its buoy lifting crane, dealt with most of these obstructions - which were worth several hundred pounds per log. As evening closed the Goodwins was beginning to swallow its latest victim and only the masts of the *Agen* were showing above the water at high tide.
In the aftermath of the gale a more fortunate ship was being towed off the shore near the South Foreland. Less than six miles distant from the ill fated *Agen*, was the Panamanian registered tanker *Sovac Radiant.* She was a large vessel of 17,598 tons which had lain broadside on, her bows into the white chalk cliffs, less than a mile from Dover. With the aid of local coastguards, who had climbed down the cliff face, and tugs, she was salved.

All that is left of the light vessel?

## *LIGHTSHIP ADRIFT*

The Goodwin Sands, famous as 'The Ship Swallower,' was about to add another to its tally of over 2000 wrecks from the past centuries. *LV 90*, or as it was known by the many ships that passed it, the *South Goodwin lightship*, was anchored very close to the wreck of the previous light vessel of the same name.

Her predecessor, the old composite *LV 69,* had probably been struck by a floating mine which had broken adrift on a rough October night in 1940. It was believed that the English mine had a safety device which rendered it harmless when washed away from its moorings. Unfortunately for the men on the anchored vessels, it was difficult to distinguish 'friend from foe' in the violent seas. Because of air attacks at the time the lightship was unmanned and luckily there were no human casualties.

With the cessation of the Second World War, crews were again allowed to man the light vessels that surrounded our coast. For many ex-merchant navy and deep-sea fishermen it was an ideal vocation. However, on the 27th of November, 1954, through the eyes of the national newspapers and a disaster, it was to become one of Britain's most dangerous jobs.

Life aboard *LV 90* was mundane and each of the seven man crew had a job to do. The master oversaw that the routine was adhered to, although he seldom had to enforce his authority. In hazy conditions, the Fog-signal Driver would be called upon to start up the massive Hornsby oil-engine to compress the air for the siren. The signal would blast out twice, through the diaphone fog-horn on every minute. Its high note would jar the nerves of a new crew member, while the low note would seem to loosen every tooth in his head. Conversation was cut to a minimum between the signals and when the weather cleared and the siren stopped the contrasting silence was as shattering as the blasting from the horn. The crews did get used to the noise and were paid tuppence an hour extra on their wages.

Along with their duties, the working watch had to keep a good lookout for ships that were passing too close to the Sands in the strong tides. When this did happen, they would hoist the two flag danger signal and fire the warning gun. These were two muzzle loading cannons with a pound and a half charge of black powder fired by a friction tube. The cannons were secured on each quarter and were always kept loaded. Every month, after a radio warning to the Coastguards, they would be fired in order to renew the charges. It would give a tremendous bang, an impressive flash of red flame, and envelope the deck in dense smoke.

Kenneth George Langham was a contented *LV 90* crew man. He had served on the *North Goodwin lightship* at the outbreak of war and, after his many years of service, had almost become used to the constant weather changes around the Goodwin Sands. The passion of the tall muscular Langham was fishing and in his spare time he would always have a line dangling from the stern of the ship. Bait would be acquired by dropping a ring net baited with old bones and bacon rind, at slack water, and catching quantities of hermit crabs.

In the autumn of 1954 cod would make up his main catch. They were always welcome and would supplement the crew's diet. Through the summer months mackerel were abundant and when cut-up and baited on a hundred hook long-line he would catch thornback ray, tope, dogfish, conger-eels and whiting. The occasional turbot would be a luxury.

Along with the autumnal weather many exhausted migratory birds would settle on the lightship's masts and rigging and, after a rest, would fly away to their destination - although many would fall foul of the vicious beaks of the large black-backed gulls.

On board the *South Goodwin light vessel* at that time was twenty-two-year-old Ronald Murton. Slightly built and softly spoken, Murton was there to study the migrating birds, as a scientist for the Ministry of Agriculture and Fisheries. On the night of November 26th the crew had warned him that they were in for some heavy weather. As the south-west wind reached storm force, the violent motion of the ship made the civil servant uncomfortable and he was unable to sleep. He put on a greatcoat over his pyjamas and struggled to the warm galley to find some company from the men off watch.

Normally conversation would have been hushed so as not to wake those who were asleep. The roar of the storm made this unnecessary and the constant seas hitting the bow cascaded volumes of water to wash over the deck. Christmas was approaching - the men's talk speculated on the size of the turkey that the Walmer lifeboat would bring them from the generous Deal townspeople. Murton hung on to his steaming mug of cocoa as the vessel pitched 'heel and toe.' Some of the crew tried to reassure him that the four ton mushroom anchor would hold them secure even in this severe gale.

As the lightship surged back on the thick anchor cable and came up with a jerk one of the chain links gave way. None of the crew had realised what had happened until the ship started to scrape along the sands. Further and further she was pushed over them, until the vessel almost made it to the other side. With the falling tide and a mountainous sea, the *LV 90* fell on to her beam ends and the Goodwins firmly grasped her. There was nothing the crew could do except to hang on to any handholds that they could find in that black and swirling maelstrom.

When the first light of day lit the scene of the tragedy, the three lifeboats from Dover, Walmer and Ramsgate were at the scene. They had been alerted by the crew of the *East Goodwin lightship* who had noticed that the 600,000 candle-power light was not flashing from its station. There was no life to be seen from the wreck and the lifeboats could not approach any closer than 700 yards.

It was an American Army Air Force helicopter, *3878*, of the Air Rescue Squadron from Manston that picked up the sole survivor, Ronald Murton. The helicopter's crew, ex-Korean war veterans, had perilously hovered so close to the lightship's hulk that they just spotted the hypothermic mans body clinging onto the light tower.

The following day heroic attempts were made by Royal Navy divers to try and discover if any more life could be found - but to no avail. The Goodwins were quickly consuming their latest victim, as the cabins and companionways were half filled with sand and would be the permanent grave of the seven crew.

Radio Caroline high and dry

Photo courtesy of *Isle of Thanet Gazette*

## *PIRATE ON THE SANDS*

The shipping forecast on Tuesday 19th November, 1991, told of increasing northeast winds. By midday the light breeze had strengthened into a gale and throughout that night and Wednesday morning it still raged. It was during those turbulent early hours that the pirate radio ship, *Ross Revenge*, had snapped her anchor cable and drifted 15 miles where she went aground on the Goodwin Sands. Until their stranding, at 4:15 a.m., the six people aboard the ship were still asleep, but when they understood their predicament they were prompt to alert the coastguard through the VHF transmitter.

The *Ross Revenge* was a retired British registered trawler, previously the German fishing vessel *Freyr,* which had plied her trade in the rough Icelandic waters, where the cod were prolific. When the Ross Fisheries Group sold her she became a wreck recovery vessel, until she was brought by Radio Caroline in 1983.

Ramsgate lifeboat promptly responded to the call, but they also ran aground in the tumultuous seas in the shallow water that surrounded to the Goodwins. For her coxswain it was one of the worst moments of his career and he was lucky to get the craft off the sand bank.

As the Dover Harbour tug, *Dextrous*, skippered by Steve Parsons, raced to the scene, he realised the Radio Caroline's caretaker crew were getting desperate. He could hear them, on the ship's radio, shouting for immediate assistance. By this time the R.A.F rescue helicopter from Manston had been scrambled and was above the wreck. They airlifted the frightened survivors from the bridge of the 30-year-old decommissioned trawler at 7:10 a.m. on that cold spume filled morning.

Meanwhile, Captain Parsons could not get his tug any closer that 900 feet from the casualty and, as he watched, the *Ross Revenge* bumped a further 600 yards across the sands. The *Dextrous* stood by, but it was not until the following day that the wind fell

light and at high water the tug managed to transport five men aboard the derelict vessel.
On channel 11 of the V.H.F radio, the Dover Coastguards issued the following warning "A wreck is stranded on the Goodwin Sands, 307 degrees from the East Goodwin Lightship, 1.8 miles."
It was just before 11 a.m. of the 21st of November that a fishing vessel from Ramsgate approached the 978 ton grounded ship. On board was Peter Murtha, a chief engineer who had worked for Radio Caroline for twenty years. He was transferred into a small rowing boat and made the perilous journey to the 210 foot long *Ross Revenge.* As he approached the hulk he alleged that he was told to 'clear off ' and that a lump of chain was thrown purposely in his direction. After re-boarding the gillnetting boat *Fairwind,* he asked, on channel 6, why he was denied access aboard a ship that he claimed was his property. The reply was that the salvage crew were acting on behalf of Dover Harbour Board and he was to contact Captain White, Dover's Harbourmaster, if he required more information. Also it was not deemed advisable or safe to try to get aboard again in his small boat. By this time, some more vessels had turned up; the angling boat *Naomi* with a TV crew and reporters plus the Dover lifeboat that offered to stand by and give assistance.
The tug's master made it quite clear that the lifeboat was there for safety and not for salvage. Information about the *Ross Revenge's* dimensions were vague and the only details that the crew and disc jockeys had given, whilst leaving the stricken hulk, was that she drew 17 feet of water. It was left up to the lifeboat to survey around the wreck and give details of the depth. Because of the tug's 14 feet draught, she could not get close enough to the ship to be of any advantage. The Dover Harbour Board boat *Diana* had arrived and was starting to pass ropes to and from the casualty. Just after mid-day Radio Caroline jingles and music were, irresponsibly and illegally, blasted out on the V.H.F working channel 6 - making communication difficult. It was decided that the tug and *Diana* should go to their private channel (45) and the airways became silent.
On Friday 22nd, the sea still remained calm and Steve Pasons was back on station in his tug *Dextrous*; also there was her sister tug, *Deft.* At 11 a.m. on the 6.8 metre high water he backed his vessel up to the wreck, which was slightly across the tide with a build up of sand on her port side. After the towing cable had been secured to the pirate radio ship's stern, Steve gunned the tug's 2,850 horse power Ruston engines (which gave her a bollard towing power of 30 tons). Much to his amazement, the hulk slid off the sands with ease and was towed into slightly deeper water. It was determined that she was to be pulled through the Kellet Gut (a gap between the Goodwin Sands) and into Trinity Bay. As the *Dextrous* towed the lifeless ship to the southwest, the *Deft* took the long way around the back of the Sands to meet up with the tow off Hope Point, near Kingsdown. By 12:30 p.m., both tugs had secured the *Ross Revenge* fore and aft and they steamed into Dover Harbour where she was moored up to the Eastern Arm half an hour later. Her Majesty's Customs closed the ship up and her owners started to negotiate a suitable sum for salvage.
December found her moved to the Granville Dock and there was a rumour that she was up for sale at £20,000. It was then reported that the owners had paid a £10,000 deposit on her the following month. In March 1992, the station manager, Peter Moore, collected quotations from towing companies to have the vessel removed to Chatham Dockyard as a tourist attraction and secure a legal license to transmit pop music. Negotiations carried on for months, with the Department of Transport taking an interest in the condition of the ship. On Thursday morning, the 27th October, 1993, the ex-Grimsby trawler was towed out of Dover Harbour and north towards the Thames estuary. The DoT had passed her seaworthy, after a refit, and her owners had paid the remaining balance on her salvage fee and harbour dues. At least the Goodwins had given this pirate a chance for redemption.

## *APPENDIX*

Position of the ***STIRLING CASTLE*** 51°-16'-30 N. 01°-30'-45 E.
Third-Rate Man-of-War. Built in 1679 by John Shish, Deptford. Length 151 feet 6 inches, Beam 50 feet. 1,087 tons. At time of loss owned by the Admiralty.
She is listed as a protected wreck site* and has an exclusion zone of 50 metres. The hull is still intact although the vessels timbers are deteriorating since she was re-exposed in 1998. Archaeology is still taking place and many of the relics can be seen in the Maritime Museum at Ramsgate.

Position of the ***ADMIRAL GARDNER*** 51°-12'-00 N. 01°-30'-46 E.
English East Indiaman. Built in 1797 by Hill and Co, London. Length 145 feet, Beam 36 feet. 816 tons. At time of loss owned by the East India Company.
This is also listed as a protected wreck site* with an exclusion zone of 150 metres. At the time of writing the Goodwin sands have yet again covered the wreck.

Position of the ***BRITISH NAVY*** 51°-14'-14 N. 01°-26'-41 E.
Full rigged iron sailing ship. Built in 1869 by Liverpool Shipbuilding Co, Liverpool. Length 206 feet, Beam 36 feet. 1,263 tons. At time of loss owned by British Shipowners Ltd.
Most of her remains lay buried in a sand bank. Along with the bell of the *Larnaca,* many dinner plates made by Cobridge, a Staffordshire potter (1870-1890), were found by the sports divers. These were part of her cargo, although most were fragmented when she was blown up by the wreck dispersal company.

Position of the ***DOLPHIN*** 51°-11'-83 N. 01°-25'-45 E.
Paddle steamer. Built in 1855 at Blackwall, London. Length 197 feet, Beam 28 feet. 641 GRT. At time of loss owned by General Steam and Navigation Co.
A very small wreck. Alfred Gann and Co of Whitstable salvaged her cargo and disposed of the ship with explosives.

Position of the ***PATRIA*** 51°-13'-02 N. 01°-25'-97 E.
Steam ship. Built in 1894 by A.G.Vulcan, Stretten. Length 460 feet, Beam 52 feet. 6,664 GRT. At time of loss owned by Hamburg Amerika Line.
Although Trinity House spent time and money clearing the wreck's remains from the shipping lane, there is still plenty of mangled ironwork left.

Position of the ***MAHRATTA*** 51°-14'-78 N. 01°-30'-05E.
Steam ship. Built in 1892 by Harland and Wolff, Belfast. Length 445 feet, Beam 58 feet. 5,730 GRT. At time of loss owned by T and J Brocklebank Line.
She is almost complete and creates a large swirl on the surface of the sea when the tide is running.

Position of the ***PREUSSEN*** 51°-08'-04 N. 01°-22'-05 E.
Five masted schooner. Built by J.C.Tecklenburg, Geeslemunde. Length 407 feet, Beam 53 feet. 5,081 GRT. At time of loss owned by Laeiz and Co.
Almost the only shipwreck in the area which can be seen above the waves at low water.

* The 'Protection of Wreck Act 1973' is to oversee historical and archaeological wrecks from interference.

Position of the ***B 2***  51°-07'-14 N.  01°-27'-58 E.
B class submarine. Built in 1905 by Vickers, Barrow in Furness. Length 150 feet, Beam 12 feet. 300 tons. At time of loss owned by the Admiralty.
This vessel is still intact apart from the collision damage. Even though she is not classed as a war grave it is hoped that divers will respect the loss of life upon her.

Position of the ***MONTROSE***  51°-14'-95 N.  01°-34'-25 E.
Steam ship. Built in 1897 by Sir Ralton Dalton and Co, Middlesbrough. Length 444 feet, Beam 52 feet. 5,195 GRT. At time of loss owned by the Ministry of War.
The ballasted hull of the *Montrose* was a focal point on the Goodwins for many years. Although she is still positioned on the chart she is seldom seen.

Position of H.M.S ***NIGER***  51°-13'-26 N.  01°-26'-38 E.
Alarm Class Torpedo Gun Boat. Built in 1892 by Vickers, Barrow-in-Furness. Length 230 feet, Beam 27 feet. 810 GRT. At time of loss owned by the Admiralty.
Although the wreck has been swept and levelled to a safe depth in the shipping lane many items of interest have been found upon her. In the past careless divers have left, on the beach, cordite that was emitted from some of her 4.7 inch shells, which was found to be still active.

Position of H.M.T ***OTHELLO II***  51°-08'-11 N.  01°-24'-60 E.
Requisitioned steam trawler. Built in 1907 by Cook, Welton and Gemmel Ltd, Beverley. Length 110 feet, Beam 22 feet. 206 GRT. At time of loss owned by the Admiralty.
This wreck is definitely a war grave as most of her crew perished with the vessel. Diving did take place in 1989 where the maker's plate was found which identified the wreck.

Position of ***THE QUEEN***  51°-08'-09 N.  01°-27'-33 E.
Requisitioned steam turbine cross Channel ferry. Built in 1903 by Denny, Dunbarton. Length 309 feet, Beam 40 feet. 1,676 GRT. At time of loss owned by the Admiralty.
It was because *The Queen* had drifted five nautical miles from her reported position that she was classified as an unknown wreck for many years. Again divers found the important clue to her identity, a small bell with the ships name upon it.

Position of the ***U-48***  51°-17'-32 N.  01°-31'-65 E.
Mobilization-class U-boat. Built 1916 by the Imperial Dockyard, Danzig. Length 213 feet. Beam 20 feet. 940 tons. At time of loss owned by the German Navy.
Apart from the damage to her stern, bow and conning tower the hull is still complete although she is no longer seen above the surface.

Position of the ***FEARLESS OF LONDON***  51°-12'-90 N.  01°-25'-44 E.
Ketch Barge. Built in 1876 by W.Colchester, Ipswich. Length 90 feet Beam, 21 feet. 108 GRT. At time of loss owned by Walter Waugh.
This wreck is not charted. All that remains of her is the cargo, 200 tons of red bricks.

Position of the ***GULL*** light vessel when she was sunk  51°-15'-85 N.  01°-28'-70 E.
Wooden Light Ship. Built in 1860. Length 103 feet. 189 tons.
At time of loss owned by Trinity House.
She now lies derelict at Grays, Essex. It is hoped to restore her, as she is the second oldest light vessel afloat.

Position of HMT ***ARAGONITE*** 51°-14'-27 N. 01°-25'-91 E.
Requisitioned steam trawler. Built in 1934 by Cook, Welton and Gemmell Ltd, Beverley. Length 133 feet, Beam 24 feet. 315 GRT. At time of loss owned by the Admiralty. There is very little left of the wreck after she was blown up and cleared by HMS *Lundy,* although the guard rails can be still be seen on what was her foredeck.

Position of the ***DUNBAR CASTLE*** 51°-22'-69 N. 01°-36'-24 E.
Passenger vessel. Built in 1930 by Harland and Wolff, Belfast. Length 471 feet, Beam 61 feet. 10,002 GRT. At time of loss owned by Union-Castle Mail SS Co.
Although this is the largest wreck in the area she seems to have almost disappeared as there is very little wreckage on the sea bed in her plotted position

Position of the ***FLANDRES*** 51°-12'-87 N. 01°-27'-25 E.
Steam ship. Built in 1914 by Akt.Ges. Weser, Bremen. Length 351 feet, Beam 43 feet. 3,611 GRT. At time of loss owned by Companie Royal Belgo Argentine.
Perhaps the excessive use of explosives caused her remains to lie over a vast area of the sea bed and is seldom viewed by divers.

Position of the ***JAMES HARROD*** 51°-13'-01 N. 01°-24'-54 E.
Liberty ship. Built in 1943 by Oregon Shipbuilding Corps, Portland. Length 441 feet, Beam 57 feet. 7,176 GRT. At time of loss owned by the American War Department.
A small amount of wreckage is all that is left of such a large ship.

Approximate position of where the ***HELENA MODJESKA*** was stranded 51°-16'-00 N. 01°-30'-00 E.
Liberty ship. Built in 1944 by Delta Shipbuilding Co, New Orleans. Length 441 feet, Beam 57 feet. 7,176 GRT. At time of loss owned by the Black Diamond Steam Ship Co.
This vessel was salved in two halves, towed to the River Blackwater and sold for scrap.

Position of the ***AGEN*** 51°-10'-70 N. 01°-31'-74 E.
Cargo vessel. Built in 1921 by W.Pickersgill and sons, Sunderland. Length 363 feet, Beam 52 feet. 4,186 GRT. At time of loss owned by Soc.Nat. des Chemmis de fer Francaise, La Rochelle.
When the tide is running the wreck causes an obstruction and the sea surface boils; although she is slowly disappearing under the sand.

Position of the ***LV 90*** 51°-14'-45 N. 01°-33'-08" E.
Light vessel. Built in 1937 by Philip and Son, Dartmouth. Length 104 feet, Beam 26 feet. 325 GRT. At time of loss owned by Trinity House Corporation.
It is debatable that the remains that can be seen are the South Goodwin lightship, although the davits that show above the sand could be those from the wreck.

Position of the ***ROSS REVENGE*** when she was stranded 51°-14'-00 N. 01°-32'-50 E.
Ex-trawler and 'Pirate radio station'. Built 1960 by AG Weser Werk, Bremerhaven. Length 210 feet, Beam 33 feet. 978 GRT. Still owned by the Radio Caroline consortium. At time of writing she is resting on the River Medway, near Rochester in Kent.

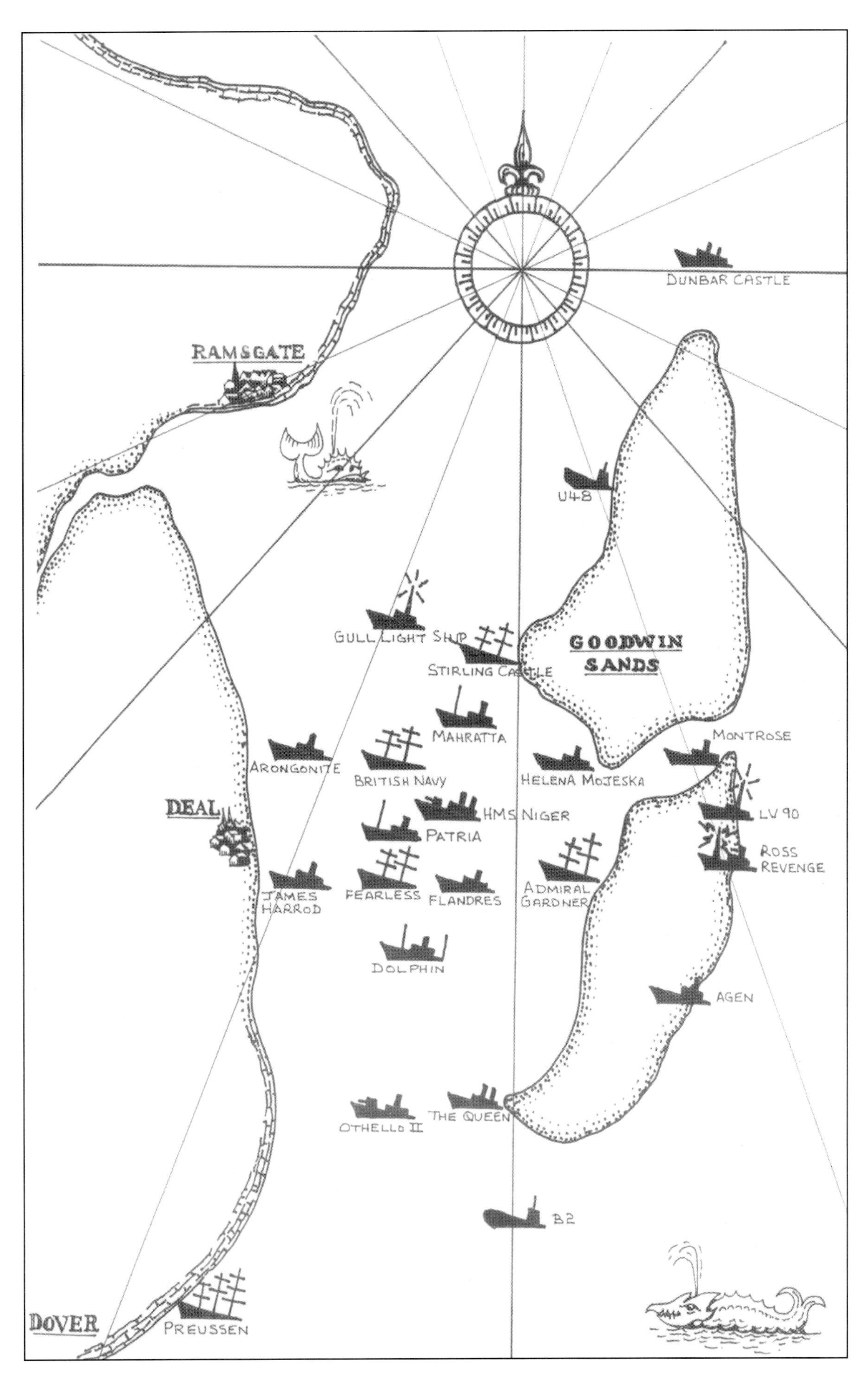
DUNBAR CASTLE
RAMSGATE
U48
GULL LIGHT SHIP
STIRLING CASTLE
GOODWIN
SANDS
MAHRATTA
MONTROSE
ARONGONITE
BRITISH NAVY
HELENA MOJESKA
DEAL
HMS NIGER
LV 90
PATRIA
ROSS
REVENGE
JAMES
HARROD
FEARLESS
FLANDRES
ADMIRAL
GARDNER
DOLPHIN
AGEN
OTHELLO II
THE QUEEN
B2
DOVER
PREUSSEN

## ACKNOWLEGMENTS:

My web site mistress Chris Knight and daughter Emma; Richard Sirot. Narrators: George Goldsmith-Carter, David Aggett, Captain Harman Heida and Captain Steve Parsons. Skippers: Allan Booth and Martin Phillips. Bob Peacock of Sea Dive. Divers: Roy Kennet, Dave Ellingworth and Paul Fletcher. Artists: Mike Crane, Terence Brind and Tom Burnham. Trinity House Corporation; Deal Library. Photographs: National Maritime Museum, Isle of Thanet Gazette and Stuart G. Smith.

**Bibliography:**

'The Goodwin Sands' (1953), Goldsmith-Carter, G.
'Seamen of the Downs' (1929), Bayley, G. B.
'Dover Patrol 1915-1917' (1932), Bacon, Sir R.
'Auxiliary Patrol' (1923), Chatterton, E. K.
'Behind the fleets' (1940), Divine, A. D.
'British vessels lost at sea 1914-18' (1919), HMSO
'British vessels lost at sea 1939-45' (1947), HMSO
'Hold the Narrow Sea' (1984), Smith, P. C.
'Allied minesweeping in WWII' (1979), Elliot, P.
'Big barges' (1983), Benham, H. & Finch, R.
'Sea surgeon' (1960), Hall OBE, J.
'Historic shipwrecks' (1998), Fenwick, V & Gale, A.
'Keepers of the sea' (1983), Woodman, R.
'The Log of a Sky Pilot' (1894), Treanor, Rev T. S.
'Deal & the Downs in the war of liberation 1939-1945', Pain, E. C.
'The Kent Coast' (1911), Lewis, A. D.

**Recommended reading:**

'The greatest storm' (2002), Brayne, M.
'The Storm' (1704) Defoe, D.
'Kent shipwrecks' (1991), Bignell, A.
'Storm Warriors'(1890), Gilmore, Rev J.
'Betwixt the Forelands' (1889), Clark Russell, W.
'Looming Lights' (1947), Goldsmith-Carter, G.
'The book of the Lifeboat' (1909), Haydon, A. L.
'The sound of the maroons (1977), Biggs, H.
'Goodwin Sands shipwrecks' (1977), Larn, R.
'Heroes of the Goodwin Sands' (1892), Treanor, Rev T. S.
'Shipwrecks of Kent' (1999), Lane, A.
'The Goodwin Sands man-of-war 1703-2003' (2002), Chamberlain, D.